D1361457

KEEPING FERRETS

ERIC FRENCH

INTRODUCTION

The ferret, or fitch as it is also known, is a relatively new arrival on the pet scene, though it has been kept by humans for probably in excess of 1,000 years. This apparent contradiction has been brought about by the fact that over much of its association with humans the ferret was, and still is, used as a hunting companion, rather than as a household pet. No doubt a number were pets, because often a sportsman may have had a need to handrear these small carnivores. However, it is only over the last couple of decades that the ferret has really taken off in a big way as an accepted household companion.

Probably more than any other pet, including the mouse or the rat, the ferret has had to overcome many prejudices in order to gain acceptance as a pet. The vast majority of stories about the ferret being a nasty tempered, foul smelling creature that would as happily bite you as look at you, are untrue. But there is rarely smoke without a fire. By having an understanding of the ferret as a species, then considering its former role and how it was managed, it can be seen how its reputation was, not surprisingly, developed. In point

Photos by Isabelle Francais through the courtesy of Nina Trischitta and the AFC Ferret Club of Long Island. Many of the ferrets shown here were loaned by Animals Alive, Ltd.

© T.F.H. Publications, Inc.

Distributed in the UNITED STATES to the Pet Trade by T.F.H. Publications, Inc., 1 TFH Plaza, Neptune City, NJ 07753; on the Internet at www.tfh.com; in CANADA by Rolf C. Hagen Inc., 3225 Sartelon St., Montreal, Quebec H4R 1E8; Pet Trade by H & L Pet Supplies Inc., 27 Kingston Crescent, Kitchener, Ontario N2B 2T6; in ENGLAND by T.F.H. Publications, PO Box 74, Havant PO9 5TT; in AUSTRALIA AND THE SOUTH PACIFIC by T.F.H. (Australia), Pty. Ltd., Box 149, Brookvale 2100 N.S.W., Australia; in NEW ZEALAND by Brooklands Aquarium Ltd., 5 McGiven Drive, New Plymouth, RD1 New Zealand; in SOUTH AFRICA by Rolf C. Hagen S.A. (PTY.) LTD., P.O. Box 201199, Durban North 4016, South Africa; in JAPAN by T.F.H. Publications. Published by T.F.H. Publications, Inc.

MANUFACTURED IN THE
UNITED STATES OF AMERICA
BY T.F.H. PUBLICATIONS, INC.

of fact, a feral cat is a far more dangerous animal than any ferret.

Ferrets are very intelligent little animals, so they respond to both kindness and cruelty. Like all carnivores, they must receive a great deal of attention while they are babies if they are to overcome their natural fear of humans. If this care is lacking the ferret will use its basic instincts in its relationship to its owners. This means it will be aggressive—and a bad tempered ferret is not an animal to treat with other than the greatest of respect. But is this not true of any pet that is equipped with an impressive dental arrangement, be this a cat, a dog, or even a tiny hamster? The difference between the ferret and these other pets is that most people are aware that cats and dogs can be extremely gentle and loving companions. They do not know this about the ferret, so its reputation is their only guide to what it is like.

In this book the true character of the ferret will be explained, as will all aspects of its management and breeding. This will give you the information you will need to determine whether or not the ferret is a pet suited to your needs. I do not suggest that this is the ideal pet for every person, but neither is a dog, a cat, a horse, or any other animal you care to think of. Each must be judged on its merits, and on the amount of care its owner is prepared to devote to it. Each has its own drawbacks as a pet, and its virtues. If you approach the subject of the ferret as a pet with an open mind, you may find it could be the perfect companion for you, or it may be a case that a dog, cat, or canary may be better. Assess the ferret on facts, not on stories handed down from past generations.

Ferrets are very intelligent animals. They are readily trained and respond to both kindness and cruelty.

Ferrets have a smooth, silky coat and have been produced in mink and sable colors with almost the same texture. They are also equipped with sharp teeth and strong jaws.

Contents

All potential pet owners should, though not all do, study their prospective companions in relation to what they are in the wild state. If this path is pursued it will tell you a great deal about the animal, and what you might reasonably expect it to be like in the confines of your home.

WHAT IS A FERRET?

The ferret is a domesticated polecat. Polecats are found throughout Europe, Asia, and the Americas. They are members of the large family of animals more well known under the common name of weasels. Some of the ferrets' wild relatives are minks, stoats, martens, wolverines, otters, badgers, skunks, and of course the very many species of weasels themselves. It is generally accepted that the domestic ferret was derived from the European polecat, *Mustela putorious*. The ferret has the scientific name of *Mustela putorious furo*. What should be appreciated with regards to the use of common names, as opposed to scientific names, is that they are rarely used in a systematic manner. For example, the European and American species *Mustela lutreola* and *M. vison* are commonly known as minks, and are more closely related to the ferret than is the marbled polecat or the African (*Zorrila*) polecat. Only one species of polecat actually carries the name of ferret, and that is the black-footed ferret (*M. nigripes*) of the USA.

Ferrets, although relatively new to the world of pets, have a long history that links them to many other animals around the world.

Common names may have a different meaning in differing countries, thus the term polecat is understood by some people in the USA to mean a skunk, as well as a weasel-like animal. There are no skunks in Europe, so the term polecat will usually refer to the ferret's wild ancestor or, more loosely, to martens and fishers. The ferret is thus a large weasel—the badgers and the wolverines being giant weasels if we apply the latter term to all members of the family Mustelidae.

THE MEANING OF NAMES

You may be interested in what the various names associated with polecats and ferrets actually mean. This will give some indication as to why the ferret has gained its various reputations. The word *Mustela* is Latin for *weasel*, while the trivial name of *putorious* is also Latin, meaning *stink*. *Furo* means *furtive* or thief-like, so putting these all together you get an animal that will readily steal, and was known to the Romans as a rather smelly weasel! The terms fitchet, foumart, fitche, and fitchew are all other common names for the pole-cat, and they are thought to be derived from the Dutch word *visse*, meaning *nasty*, or from the descriptive term *foul marten*. The term *polecat* came from the Middle English word *polcat*, which in turn is thought to have come from the French words *poule* (chicken) and *chat* (cat). Thus the *poule chat* was a cat-like animal that killed chickens.

In all of these instances the polecat is not regarded in the most favored light, this re-

Prairie dogs are distantly related to ferrets.

Polecats, which we call *ferrets*, practice mutual cleaning in their native habitat.

flecting its stealth and ability to steal from farms. When cornered it will not hesitate to release its defensive odor, thus the association with nasty smells—much in the same manner that the skunk will. The skunk's common name, when used in the human context, implies an underhanded person, as does the term *weasel* itself. There is a long history of associating the polecat, and later the ferret, with less than desirable attributes.

FERRET FEATURES

The ferret is very typical of the weasel family, having a long and sinuous body that enables it to move through burrows and other small tunnels with ease. In total length the adult will range from 44-60cm (17-24in) in length, the male being larger than the female. Of this length almost half is made up

Like other members of the weasel family, the ferret has a long and sinuous body.

of its tail. The average weight is 1.1-2.5kg (2.4-5.5lb). A large ferret is about half the weight of the average medium sized cat. Its weight will vary during the course of a year. Its digits are 5/5 meaning five

Did you know ferrets have more teeth than cats? Also, half their length is made up of their tails.

toes on each foot.

The dental arrangement in the ferret is on similar lines to that found in many carnivores. The permanent teeth are preceded by milk or deciduous teeth. The adult has a total of 34 teeth, compared to 30 in the cat and 42 in the dog. The most specialized teeth of all carnivores are the canine, or 'eye' teeth which are elongated, and set on either side of the incisor teeth. They are of course used in killing their prey. The dental formula of the ferret is:

$$\frac{3-1-3-1}{3-1-3-2} = \frac{1}{2} \text{ jaw} = 34$$

The formula quoted is typical for the species, but not necessarily for all individuals because, as in most species, anomalies are quite common. In ferrets, an individual may have more incisors than is typical for the species as a whole.

The ferret has no caecum, indicating its carnivorous diet. Data on its reproductive features are given in the appropriate chapter. Under normal conditions you can expect your ferret to live for about 6-8 years, though it may well attain 10 or more years if conditions are very favorable (correct diet and little stress).

An important feature of ferrets are the scent glands. These are situated on either side of the anal canal. They are both defensive and sexual indicators. They are used to release a pungent smell which is offensive to would-be attackers. Unlike the skunk, which can spray this liquid, the ferret cannot. Even so, it can act as a strong deterrent to those, such as the dog or fox, which might attempt to bite it. It is this smell, of course, that has given rise to the unwarranted reputation of these animals for being smelly. In reality, the ferret will not release the fluid unless it is frightened—nor indeed will a skunk. However, when a ferret does release its scent it will linger, and it is this, rather than the initial smell, that people may find offensive. The same is true of the scent of the skunk, which is not foul smelling, just a powerful musk. The trail left by the scent of a polecat is used rather in the manner of a calling card. Other animals are able to obtain information as to the sex and physical state of the owner.

Both of the ferret sexes have a characteristic body odor, the male more so than the female. The same is true of male mice, cats, dogs, and most other pets. This whole question of odor will be discussed in more detail in relation to *ferrets as pets* in a later chapter.

It is worth noting in respect of reputations, that many people will comment on the scent of a skunk, yet they have never even been close to this very cute little carnivore. Even the wild skunk does not spray without giving ample indication that this is a distinct possibility if you do not leave it alone. The same is true of the ferret, but reputations will be passed from one person to another without the people involved having any actual experience of the animal they denigrate. This said, the ferret, like the tom cat, may mark its territory by scenting, but the scent is less pungent than that of the polecat.

The ferret has very keen senses, as must any animal that survives by hunting. Its vision is fair, while its hearing, especially in the higher pitches, is much better. Without doubt its finest sense is that of smell, which is used to track down its prey. It is a very inquisitive little animal, much like a cat, and this aspect of its nature, which is really a hunting instinct, becomes quite amusing when transposed to the domestic situation.

In the wild the ferret is a fearless hunter—a reputation it shares with most members of its family. There are few animals of its own, and even larger, size that it will not tackle. Its method of killing is usually a bite at the base of the cranium. The canine teeth are extremely sensitive at their tips and can 'feel' for the correct place to sink the fangs. If they did not do this there would be the obvious risk that the teeth could be damaged if they bit into bone. An alternative bite is at the throat, but this is not commonly used at it is not without risk from the raking action of its prey's front feet—or from their teeth if the ferret's judgment is not precise.

The range of prey of the ferret is quite wide. Its main victims are rabbits, mice and other small mammals. It will take birds when it can—these including domestic stocks such as chickens, which has not endeared it to farmers. Various reptiles and amphibians, such as small snakes and frogs, comprise the largest part of the diet after mammals. Fish and invertebrates (worms, beetles and their like) may also make up a sizable part of the menu, depending on the season and locality the ferret lives in.

The ferret is not beyond eating carrion if this has only recently died, or been killed by some other predator. Like most predators, the ferret will tend to be more proficient at killing one type of prey than another. This comes through practice, and will often result in the animal seeking out that prey to the exclusion of others. Once a ferret has become used to the easy pickings on a farm, it can become a source of considerable damage to the poultry farmer—made the more of a problem because the ferret is able to gain entry via holes that would not allow a fox to enter.

On the credit side, a ferret may help in keeping down the rodent population, as well as

A close relative of the ferret is the badger, *Meles meles.*

Domesticated skunks compete with ferrets as pets and many color varieties have been domestically produced.

from about the first century, and the ferret was used at that time in helping to catch wild specimens. The Normans are credited with introducing rabbit gardens, or coneygarths, into Britain about the 12th century. All feudal lords of the period maintained rabbit colonies, and they also kept ferrets. Given these various facts it would seem probable that the ferret began its path of domestication in southern Europe, possibly about 100BC.

One of the earliest illustrations of the ferret is seen on a Psalter that is dated circa 1325. During the 15th century the ferret is depicted in numerous paintings and tapestries, and during this time the rabbit's popularity was growing throughout Europe. The two are intrinsically linked. It is also noted

The short-clawed otter is related to the ferret, though it has not been domesticated as a house pet.

Photo courtesy of Colour Library.

that of lagomorphs—rabbits and hares. The full impact of ferrets in a rural situation is often beneficial, but a few rogue specimens quickly give the predator an unjust reputation. The situation is common to many hunters, such as cats, foxes, and their like. One of the problems is that man invariably hunts a predator's normal prey almost to extinction, so the predator has little option but to seek food wherever it can, and this means on farms.

DOMESTIC HISTORY

As with many other domesticated species, the history of the ferret is very uncertain. In the absence of documented evidence all that can be done is to draw premises from the history of happenings that may have pertained prior to the first authenticated records of these animals. It has been suggested that the Egyptians were the first people to keep ferrets in 500 BC in order to combat the mouse problem in their granaries. This seems unlikely on the grounds that

the Egyptians always mummified, and depicted on tombs and ceramics, all of the animals that were common at that time.

This was especially so in relation to any creatures that were useful to them, or which formed part of a deity. There appears to be no such records of ferrets. Further, 1500 BC would almost have predated the arrival of the cat into the major divinities of Egypt. It seems more likely that the ferret would come onto the domestic scene when it had a very obvious practical use— and it is doubtful if this would have been in connection with mice. A more realistic role would have been in connection with rabbiting. If this is accepted, it might possibly have been used in Spain, where the ancestors of domestic rabbits may have come from. The rabbit did not appear in Britain until about the 12th century, though some authorities believe they may have arrived earlier via the Romans. The Romans are known to have kept rabbits

Photo by Robert Pearcy.

Raccoons have become interesting house pets and several books have been written about keeping them as pets.

that the illustrations of the ferret from as early as the 15th century are of albinos.

From the Middle Ages until the early years of this century the ferret was very much a part of the rural setting. All large landowners had their gamekeepers, and these kept ferrets in order to try to keep the number of rabbits in check. The ferret was also a major player in the 'sport' of rabbit hunting, both for the pleasure this provided, and for the meat that would result for the pot. Farmers were also ferreters—and there was no shortage of poachers. Thousands of both town and countryfolk in England, as well as throughout Europe, kept a number of ferrets in order to help supplement the meager rations that were the poor man's lot until comparatively recent times.

The ferret was taken to the USA during the 19th century

The Canadian otter is a close relative of the ferret. They are very interesting and playful when they are young but they have not been domesticated.

in order to help reduce the rodent populations. Likewise, it was exported (along with stoats and weasels) to both Australia and New Zealand to combat the rampant rabbit populations. However, it failed in this task because too much was expected of it. In Europe the ferret (or more appropriately the polecat) is but one of many predators that kill rabbits, but in Australia and New Zealand there are less predators (including birds of prey), so the ferret had little impact on the vast numbers of rabbits.

In reality, other predators, such as feral and wild cats, would have more success in keeping down rabbit populations simply because they would consume more of the young. The ferret's asset is in catching rabbits, or rather bolting them from their burrows, rather than as population regulators per se.

With the improvement in the

working man's lot that became evident as the 20th century got underway, there was a decline in the need for many people to use ferrets in order to catch rabbits for the pot. During this period other things were changing too. The large landowners were finding it more costly to maintain their lands, much of which were sold. This reduced the number of gamekeepers, thus the number of ferrets. Chemicals and gassing were used to exterminate rabbits on a large scale.

Finally, the dreaded rabbit disease, myxomatosis, wreaked havoc with rabbit populations all over the world. This had a two-fold effect. It saw the sale of rabbit meat plummet, and it drastically affected the sport of rabbiting. All of these happenings did no favors for the ferret, whose numbers fell dramatically. They have never recovered in terms of rabbiting, and compared to former years only a very small number of people now participate in this pastime.

Where the ferret was found to have a new use was in laboratories, as well as in commercial fitch farms that bred the ferret for its fur. However, fitch, or ferret fur, never really caught on, though farms still exist in Denmark and New Zealand in particular, with others dotted about the globe. The ferret was also used in a limited manner as a ratter, but this is not a role it is well suited to. A large rat is well able to give a ferret more than a good fight, so terriers were much more commonly used in this role, even by those who owned ferrets.

THE FERRET'S BAD REPUTATION

As you can see, the ferret has had a very long association with humans, so it is perhaps surprising that its reputation was, for such a long period, a bad one. However, when you consider how it was invariably kept and treated, it is all too obvious just why this reputation was acquired. As with just about all domestic animals our knowledge of them really only started to become in depth in modern times. For most, possibly excluding the dog, they were greatly misunderstood. The working ferret was often starved before it was sent down a burrow in the mistaken belief that it would work better. In other instances its canine teeth were broken so it could not kill the rabbit. Others had their lips temporarily sewn together, or they were fitted with tight muzzles. Some were actually blinded, all in the belief that this would prevent them from harming the rabbit.

Less physically cruel, but actually almost as bad, was the practice of fitting bells to the ferret. The obvious notion was that it warned the rabbit of the oncoming ferret (as if the rabbit would not be aware of this by its own powerful sense of smell).

The bell seems a sound enough idea until you stop to appreciate that many a ferret did not come out of the burrow, so was left by its owner. Fitted with a bell it had little chance of catching any prey, so would have to subsist on carrion and invertebrates, or starve to death, which no doubt many did. Sometimes the bell could be heard by the owner who would then dig away in the hope of recovering the ferret, but this did not always happen. The dig could also bury the poor animal. At this juncture it will become apparent to those who know nothing of rabbiting that the object of the ferret is not to kill the rabbit, but to frighten it out of its burrow—hence into the purse or catch net of the hunter who would then dispatch it, or whose dogs would kill it should it avoid the net.

Once back home the ferret would be placed into a small cage and given only a Spartan diet, such as the entrails from the rabbits, some bread and milk, and kitchen scraps. It received little consideration on those very hot or cold days, for the ferret pens were often totally inadequate homes with little insulation— much as many rabbit hutches used to this day are inadequate for the pets that are forced to live in them.

All in all, for most ferrets, life was hardly a bed of roses!

Given the way they were treated it is no surprise to find that they were not slow in trying to bite the hand of their tormentors. This would result in the owner using heavy gloves, which have little sense of feel to them. A strong grip would be placed on the poor wretch which was then either placed in a box or a sack. In this fearful state the ferret would obviously release its scent, so you now have a very aggressive and frightened animal—thus the smelling, biting reputation.

It should be stated that not all owners treated their ferrets in this manner—but enough did to foster the animal's reputation. Further, it was considered 'macho' to tell your friends just what a nasty bit of goods your ferrets were, yet boast how super they were as rabbiters. Those who treated their ferrets with consideration were often the butt of scorn or jokes. Yet the well cared for ferret was a superior working animal. The same is true of a caring shepherd, who will get far more work from his dogs than one who uses a heavy hand, and the half starvation principle, notions that such people never apply to themselves!

THE PET FERRET

By reviewing the domestic history of the ferret it is easily seen why it has been unfairly judged. The steady growth in its popularity as a pet bears testimony to the fact that it can be gentle, amusing, and in every way a quite delightful pet. Once you own a ferret you will be mystified as to why people could have so badly misjudged this little bundle of fur for so many years.

With some understanding of the wild and domestic history of the ferret we can now look specifically at the advantages, and also the possible negatives, to having a ferret as a household pet. No pet is ideally suited to every person, and anyone who tells you otherwise knows little about animals, and even less about people. Much depends on the disposition of the owner, their circumstances in respect to available time, and of course their particular likes and dislikes. In straight comparison terms, and having owned just about every type of pet from a monkey to a mouse,

I would say that the ferret as a pet compares more to a cat than to any other animal you might choose from.

HOME SUITABILITY

In some ways the ferret is better suited to the majority of homes than the cat. This is because I have never considered a cat suited to apartment life, whereas the ferret is. It has a similar attitude to its owner—one of loving, yet retaining its own individuality. By this is meant that a ferret, like a cat, will come to you if it feels inclined to do so—if not it will totally ignore your calls. More so than a cat,

it can be both mischievous, and rather expert at getting into places it shouldn't. You do not expect a dog to clamber into a washing machine, but both a cat and a ferret will if they think it seems a good idea at the time! Usually they will promptly curl up in a ball and go to sleep. The difference is that a cat is a very light sleeper, the ferret is the opposite. This difference no doubt reflects the fact that a ferret normally sleeps deep in a burrow where it is unlikely to be disturbed.

Cats have a habit of jumping onto any surface from a chair to a table, and ferrets are of the same manner. They are not actually good jumpers, but will often find some way to clamber up things in order to investigate every part of their environment. So, if you think you would find a cat a bit of a nuisance to your highly organized way of living, it is probable the ferret will affect you in much the same, or an even greater, manner.

Ferrets enjoy being with their owners for as much time as possible. They become better pets the more time you spend with them. This is actually very important in ferret owning. The cat that is infrequently handled is unlikely to bite. In fact, cats rarely have a need to bite, given the pain they can inflict with their claws. The ferret that is not frequently handled is more likely to nip when it is picked up. This is a fact of life that some people play down when discussing the merits of ferrets.

A ferret is not a good choice as a pet if you have very young children in the home. They are not as forgiving of

The ferret, when well bred and well treated, becomes a lovable, adorable pet.

rough handling as are dogs, and, to a lesser extent, cats. If a toddler grabs a ferret and hurts it, you can count on the ferret hurting the toddler in most instances. Sadly, a lot of pet ferret owners do go out and purchase the cuddly kits on impulse, only to find they are not quite what they expected. The ferret is then either abandoned in the country, a most inconsiderate way to treat any animal, or it is sold to another, probably unsuitable, person looking for a nice unusual pet.

TRANSPORTING FERRETS

One very useful attribute of the ferret is that it can easily be transported in a shopping bag, or even a large coat pocket, assuming it is trained to this from a young age. There are not many pets this can be said of. Unlike most cats, it will enjoy a romp in the country—but of course must never be let off its lead. Many owners actually take their ferrets for a walk in the park, but a degree of caution is advised when dogs are seen.

EASE OF FEEDING

The ferret is very cosmopolitan in its dietary needs. It eats less than a cat, so it is not an expensive pet to feed. Its nutritional needs are discussed in detail in a later chapter, but here we can establish that this will create no problems at all to you.

Personal Cleanliness. The ferret is comparable to a cat in the way it fastidiously cleans itself. Its fur is short, so it never gets into a mess. It requires little if any grooming. There is no need to bathe a ferret, though many owners

> Ferrets are not pets for very young children. If you have a child in the house, both ferret and child should become acquainted under your supervision.

do. However, if it is bathed from a young age it will accept this indignity with quiet indifference, as long as you handle it gently.

Gregarious Nature. Although the wild polecat is rather a solitary creature the same is not as true for the ferret. During the course of domestication a number of changes occur within an animal species. These are what make it domesticated. The animal becomes less excitable, it has less desire to escape captivity, and its sexual drives are reduced. The extent of these reduced traits are variable, and are also influenced by the environment a pet lives in. Ferrets will live amicably with their own kind, and will happily befriend a dog or cat, the latter being more suited to their temperament. Of course, it would be very unwise to allow your pet ferret to ap-

proach your pet rabbit, guinea pig, mouse, hamster or bird. These are all its natural prey. While any animal can be imprinted with another species, this should not be attempted with pets. The ferret would have no qualms about killing any of these other animals.

NEED FOR CONFINEMENT

The ferret owner cannot allow his pet free access to the outdoors, as can be done with cats. This is because the ferret would quickly be off investigating its surroundings and would probably get lost. Their homing instinct is not especially good. Further, the average person is not familiar with a ferret and might attempt to kill it thinking it was some potentially dangerous animal.

Within most neighborhoods there will be those who may keep aviary birds, pigeons, rabbits, or similar pets. A ferret on the loose could cause disorder—should it gain entry to their enclosures—which would not make you the most popular person on the block. The ferret owner

ferrets

must therefore be especially diligent in hot weather when doors or windows might be left open. Suitable indoor or outdoor accommodations are thus essential so that the ferret can be confined when there is a need to do so. This could of course be in a room.

HOUSETRAINING

The ferret is easily housetrained to use a litter tray in much the same way as a kitten is. It is very clean in its toiletry habits as long as it is given the opportunity to be so. This must be done as soon as it is acquired. This aspect is discussed in the following chapter.

Choice of Colors. The majority of people think in terms of ferrets as being albinos, that is, all white with pink eyes. However, there are numerous alternative colors and patterns that you can choose from, and the number is rising. These are discussed

Ferrets are not toys for children. The ferret must be caged when the children have access to them.

in a later chapter, together with basic genetics for those who might ultimately be interested in color breeding with these pets.

THE QUESTION OF ODOR

The ferret has a characteristic body odor. To what degree you would find this offensive is obviously a matter of personal thoughts. I like the smell of horses, but another person may not. With a ferret you can overcome, to an almost complete degree, its odor if you so wish. Both the hob (male) and the jill (female) can have their anal glands surgically removed, as well as their reproductive organs, in order to remove almost all traces of body odor. This is certainly advisable in the case of the jill, and not for any reasons of odor, but purely for her own good health.

The hob is normally castrated for the same reasons that you may have desexed your tom cat. It reduces their desire to mark their territory, and also makes them a little more placid.

Biting. Contrary to popular belief, ferrets are not aggressive animals if they have no need to be. If they are correctly and regularly handled from babies they will not bite. Of course, like any young animal, whether it be a puppy, a kitten, a parrot, or a pony, they will nip you until they learn this is not the proper thing. All babies, including humans, go through a biting stage as they learn about what is and is not acceptable behavior. Ferrets enjoy a rough and tumble with their littermates, and bite each other in the process. This is natural behavior and

when you obtain one it will only do what it has always done. However, such nips are not in anger (if they were it could bite you almost to the bone). If the ferret is handled gently, and taught not to bite (which is explained under general care) it will not do so. Those who own biting ferrets either did not rear them correctly from babies, purchased an adult that was not trained, or obtained a ferret from the wrong source. The ferret, as stated previously, is no different to a cat, a dog, a parrot or other pet. You will get out of it only what you put into it.

For some reason people seem to think that ferrets are born bad tempered, which just is not the case. What is the truth is that they are a pet that needs a lot of attention. If this is not possible in your household you should not even consider owning a ferret—it really is that simple. The ferret can give you endless hours of enjoyment because it really does love life.

It enjoys being tickled, stroked and caressed. It enjoys climbing over its owner and going to sleep wrapped around his or her neck. It is lovingly mischievous, and it is intelligent. It is no problem to look after, and will not be out annoying your neighbors by barking as with unruly dogs— nor be shrieking at the top of its voice, as will many of the larger parrots. It will not be roaming the neighborhood calling for queens as do most unneutered tom cats, and it will not stare at you with a blank expression as will a tank full of goldfish. All in all its credentials are rather good wouldn't you say?

The housing that you provide for your ferret(s) will fall into one of two basic types. There is that for the household pet, and that for ferrets kept outdoors. Which you choose will probably be determined by whether or not you plan to breed your ferrets. I would not recommend you even consider breeding until you have gained some practical experience with ferrets. Most readers will be thinking of obtaining one or two ferrets as household pets, so we will discuss the housing needs of these first.

INDOOR ACCOMMODATION

Owners of ferrets, as with any other pet, have their own ideas on what sort of accommodation they would like their pets to have, or how much they are prepared to spend on this. You will find that whatever arrangements you provide for the ferrets they will invariably make up their own minds whether they deem it suitable. This is especially true where their sleeping quarters are concerned.

Like cats, ferrets will tend to sleep wherever seems appropriate to the moment. This means it could be in that which you have provided for them, on a chair, in a basket of clothes waiting to be washed, or on your bed. It could also be in an open drawer, or on top of the floor

heater vent—as one of ours does during the colder winter months.

In the wild, ferrets sleep in burrows. These have their own food and toilet rooms, as well as the main sleeping area. You should provide

Don't try this with a ferret you don't know! The more you handle your ferret the more accepting he will be of your attention.

similar arrangements, though not of course in a burrow. The need to housetrain the ferret is an aspect that should affect the initial freedom your pet is given. It may also determine the ultimate freedom the pet is given over any 24-hour period.

THE FERRET CAGE

It is recommended that you construct a good ferret cage in advance of obtaining your pet. This should be spacious, but need not be especially so if the ferret is to be given a great deal of time outside of the cage. If it is to be used purely as a place of temporary confinement its size could be of the order of 93x46x46cm (36x18x18cm). This will allow you room to place in it a cozy sleeping box, food dishes, and a latrine tray. The height allows you to fix the sleeping box in a raised position, and entered via a stepping block, or short solid ladder type walkway.

The cage is best made from weldwire with a 2.5x2.5cm (1x1in) hole size and of a gauge (thickness) not less than 19. This hole size will not permit the ferret to escape the cage, while the gauge quoted is reasonably stiff (but a lower size would be stiffer, thus better). You can purchase weldwire panels that can be clipped together, and these allow you to make the cage any size you deem suitable.

Alternatively, you could assemble a wooden frame and staple the weldwire onto the inner edges of this, being sure to trim off any sharp pieces where you have cut the wire— or you can cover these with aluminum. The wood should

be well coated with a good gloss paint so it can be easily wiped clean. You can purchase either plastic or epoxy coated weldwire and these look smarter. The latter is easily the better choice because ferrets, especially babies, may bite pieces of plastic from the wire. If these were swallowed they might very well create an internal blockage.

The cage could have either a front or top opening door, the latter being a good choice as it saves you bending down quite as far. Be sure the door is large enough to allow the litter critter to pass through it. The base of the cage is best made from stiff plastic or aluminum sheeting as this is much easier to keep clean. Wood absorbs urine and will soon begin to smell. You could use wood if this was first painted and then covered with stiff plastic that was screwed into place. By adopting the latter approach the plastic can be removed periodically to give the whole thing a good clean. If plastic is used be sure this is fitted such that the ferrets cannot easily get their teeth onto the edge—which will promptly start to rip.

Behind the area where the litter tray will be placed it is also useful to place a plexiglass (perspex) splashback to ensure no urine is deposited outside the cage. The sleeping box can be made from plastic, or one of the laminated woods that are easy to clean. If the entrance side, or top, is hinged this will make for easy cleaning. The entrance itself should be a hole just above the floor level (or in the roof) and about 7.5cm (3in) in diameter. It should be placed to one side

of center so that there is ample room for the ferret to curl up in without being in front of the hole. Place the hole in the long side of the oblong box.

The size of the box is not important as long as it is large enough to accommodate the ferret, or two if this is how many pets you have. It needs to be roomy, yet not so large that it is not snug. The latrine should be made of plastic or aluminum. The sides should be large enough to prevent the floor litter from falling out, but not so deep that the ferret has difficulty in getting into it. You can use cat litter, or sawdust and wood shavings, for the base covering. These should be of suitable depth to soak up the urine.

If the ferret is likely to have to spend long periods in the cage then it should be made larger, so it affords a good area for it to exercise in. There were no commercially made ferret cages for pet owners, but now there are really nice large and hygienic indoor pens you are recommended to purchase which are economical, yet roomy walk in indoor aviary flights. Some of these even feature casters so you can easily move the pen from one room to another.

They are eminently suitable for ferrets. With such a unit you can place logs and walkways in them in order to utilize the height. Platforms can also be incorporated so a really interesting, yet very practical, cage is the result. You will also see many large cages that would prove suitable for ferrets.

Another alternative that you may find suitable is to

use a puppy playpen as indoor accommodation. These come in various sizes and can be purchased at dog shows—or you could easily make your own by fitting weldwire onto a wooden frame. The panels thus produced can be of any size to suit your needs. In the playpen you can then place the sleeping box, litter tray, and food containers. The height of the panels should be about 76cm (30in). By placing a short ledge of a few inches depth along the top of the panels you will be sure the ferrets cannot escape by climbing up and over the edge. The advantage of the playpen is that it provides the ferrets with more room, and is relatively inexpensive to purchase or construct.

PLAYTHINGS

The ferret is a very inquisitive creature so responds very well to playthings. Among the items that are favored are tubes of various diameters. These can be glued together in order to create a small maze of tunnels that the ferret will really enjoy clambering through. Some could be made of clear plastic, with others in a standard gray (which can always be painted with colors to blend in with those of your room).

Small blocks of wood, as well as items dangling from string, after the fashion of cat scratching posts with things hanging from them, will all amuse your ferret. Climbing frames are another item that a ferret will really enjoy. Cover them with carpeting, and do be sure the ferret can come down them as easily as it can clamber up them. They are not jumpers, so must have the means to come down things easily. Suitable balls will amuse them for short periods, but be sure they are not the sort that the ferret can tear pieces from. Dog chews may also amuse them, and will provide good exercise for their jaw muscles.

HOUSETRAINING

It is very important that from the outset you housetrain your pet. This is why a cage is such a useful unit, because it quickly trains the ferret to use its litter tray. Once the habit has been acquired, one or more trays can be placed in strategic rooms so that when your pet is free roaming it will auto-matically seek a litter tray when it needs to relieve itself. If this approach is not adopted the result will be that the ferret will find what it considers to be the best place to use as a toilet, and will thereafter foul that corner of a

Ferrets love to examine dark tunnels...like a large shoe. Be careful they don't use a shoe as their private lavatory.

Ferrets can be housetrained...like cats...to use a litter tray. They are not pleasant pets unless they are housetrained.

room—with the resulting build up of odors.

OUTDOOR ACCOMMODATION

If you decide that you wish to keep your ferrets outdoors then the options will range from a sound hutch, to utiliz-ing a shed or other outbuild-ing. If you eventually decide to become a breeder you will need a range of units. In this instance considerable thought should be placed into the design of the breed-ing unit so that you are able to provide practical yet inter-esting homes for your ferrets. Do remember that when a large number of ferrets are planned, you may

need special permissions to keep these, and for any buildings that might be regarded as being of a permanent type.

Likewise, any utilities, such as water, sewage, and electric, which is supplied to outdoor structures, should be installed correctly, and may also need local planning consents. Another aspect that must always be considered when housing a number of ferrets in an outdoor situation is that of your neighbor's thoughts. With just one or two pets they are not likely to be overly concerned. If the numbers kept are greater than this they might consider these to be an annoyance (if the housing was not kept clean for example). Any neighbors who keep rabbits or aviary birds tend to get very edgy if they know there is a ferret breeder in the vicinity.

It is best to be on good terms with such neighbors so they are not likely to complain about your activities to the local authorities. Of course, this works two ways if they are breeding animals them-selves, it's just that few people object to aviary birds, but they may worry about ferrets getting loose, especially if they do not know that these are not dangerous to them.

HUTCHES

At the bottom of the out-door housing list is the simple hutch. Of necessity these are made of wood because of the need to insulate them from variable weather conditions. The most important aspect, and one often badly neglected by many animal keepers, is to ensure that even a simple hutch is very well con-structed. You cannot utilize the small flimsy hutches sold in petshops to house a ferret, or any other animal unless it is in an indoor situation. Even then they will not do the job adequately.

Such hutches reflect con-sumer demand for inexpen-sive units, not the suitability of such units to actually house pets in. If you cannot provide adequate outdoor accommodation then do not keep a ferret outdoors, be-cause you will condemn it to a life of misery.

Dimensions: The outdoor hutch should be of good dimensions, and a length of 93cm(36in) would be about the minimum. The depth should be in the order of 45cm(18in), with a height of at least 38cm(15in). This can be divided into three sections. At one end there will be a sleeping area of about 15cm (6in) wide, with a similar sized room at the opposite end that will be the latrine. The space between these rooms will be the feeding and exercise area. Both can be entered via pop holes situated a few centime-ters above the floor. To faci-litate ease of cleaning both should have hinged exterior doors.

Materials: It is best to use solid timber that is about 1.25cm (1/2in) thick. This

can be tongue and grooved marine ply, or any similar timber. If it is placed on a solid frame you can then line this with a thinner board and pack insulating material between the two walls. You now have a really solid struc-ture that will withstand both low and high temperatures.

The front of the exercise area should be of weldwire stapled onto a frame. The hole size of the wire should be 2.5x2.5cm (1x1in). This frame can be hinged to make clean-ing easy, or it can be slotted down runners so that it is easily removed. If you coat the weldwire with bitumen this will look better, and add extra life to it. All of the timber used in the construction should be well treated with a preserva-tive and allowed to dry thor-oughly before any ferrets are introduced into the hutch.

> Your local pet shop will have cages suitable (large enough) for a ferret.

The Roof: The roof should have a slope to it in order to take rain away. It should also overhang the side walls to give them some protection. It can be covered with a suitable roofing felt for added protec-tion.

Supports: The hutch should be raised above floor level in order that there is a good air circulation beneath the hutch floor. This can be effected by placing it on cinder (breeze) blocks. Better still would be to have it on solid legs that form part of the hutch framework. This will be more attractive.

Exterior Floor: In order that the hutch surrounds can be maintained in a really clean state it is advisable to stand the hutch on either a concrete base, or one of slabs.

Interior Protection: To protect the interior hutch walls and floor from general dirt, and urine in particular, they are best treated with a number of coats of paint. You could also place rigid plastic on the latrine walls and this will greatly reduce the possibility of odors.

Protection From Winds: The weldwire section can be protected from cold winds by having a detachable rigid clear plastic cover. This can be held in place by hooks and swivel latches. Leave an opening at the top of about an inch or so in order that air can circulate into the hutch. You might also feature a few holes high up in the latrine area in order that fresh air can circulate. These will be protected from rain by the roof overhang. The hutch should be sited where it has some protection from inclement weather, also where it is not exposed to direct sunshine throughout the day. Ferrets suffer badly when the temperature starts to climb past the 70°F mark. In the wild they would normally be fast asleep in their cool burrows—venturing out at dusk in order to feed.

Floor Covering: This can be of a sawdust base on which quality straw or hay is added. An alternative is to use granulated paper, which is both hygienic and does not cling as much to food items. Hay will provide a cozy bedding material, but should not be used for nursing jills as it can get too hot. Hay must be of very good quality, never damp or with a musty smell. This can create fungal prob-

lems. Wood shavings are another option.

The hutch described will provide your ferret with a really sound home that will keep it warm in the cold weather, and cooler in the hot periods. It will last almost for a lifetime if it is regularly treated with preservatives. Such a hutch does not allow the ferret adequate exercise area, so it is assumed that you will take the ferret indoors on a regular basis.

HUTCH AND EXERCISE AREA

If the ferret is not to be taken indoors too often, apart from the fact it will not make such a good pet, you should place the hutch in an enclosed area to provide plenty of exercise. The ideal arrangement is to place the hutch into an aviary structure so there is no chance that it can escape. This will also be easier for you to enter and stand upright in. Such a covering can then have rocks, piping, and other playthings added so that the ferret can really enjoy its confined existence.

Whenever an outdoor exercise area is prepared it is important to sink the wire perimeter fence at least 31cm (12in) into the ground. It should then be turned at right angles and continue back into the run area for a similar distance. This greatly reduces the risk of the ferret burrowing out of the enclosure. The alternative strategy is to site the enclosure on a concrete bed, or slabs. An earth mound can then be added, and sewage or other pipes placed into this so as to create a tunnel system that the ferret will play in.

The hutch can have one modification in order that the ferret can come and go as it pleases. Towards the back wall of the exercise part of the hutch, in the floor, you can feature a 7.5 cm (3in) or more diameter hole. From this you can place a sloping ramp to the outside floor. Place wooden struts across this so the ferret will not be at risk of sliding. When erecting outdoor enclosures it is best to have at least two ferrets so that they provide company for each other.

USING AN OUTBUILDING

A very satisfactory home can be provided for a number of ferrets if a shed or other outbuilding is utilized. The shed itself can provide excellent indoor accommodation, whilst an outdoor run could then be added along the lines already described. The shed itself can feature a number of sleeping boxes of various sizes, depending on how many ferrets are to be accommodated.

The boxes are best sited a foot or more above ground level and approached via wide planks or similar ramps. Litter trays can be placed near the exit door, with food receptacles some way from these. It is useful if the shed door is of the stable type so that the top half can be opened on warm days. Alternatively, you could feature an internal weldwire door so that this can be opened to let fresh air in, whilst restricting the ferrets to the shed if you did not want them in the exercise area for any period of time.

The floor of the shed should be of concrete or slabs, duly covered with a generous layer

of wood shavings. Failing this, should it be of wood, cover this with a good linoleum or plastic tiles that are easily cleaned. The shed can contain numerous additions. These can include a pile of rocks, various large logs, and climbing frames. If there is no outside run you could feature an earth mound with pipes in it. All of these things will make for a really interesting home for your pets. The shed should contain at least one good sized window in it so that plenty of light enters the building. Cover this with weldwire on the inside so that in the summer you can leave the window open for fresh air, with no risk that an unusually adventurous ferret could devise a way to get out.

The shed walls are best covered with suitable lining boards so a smooth surface is created, and which can be painted in a light color. This will be easy to keep clean. Insulating material could also be placed in the wall cavity thus formed. It is certainly useful if you can include an electric supply to the shed for lighting, and maybe even a sink with a water supply. This will make cleaning chores much more enjoyable. Heating is not needed if the sleeping boxes are nicely filled with nesting material. Very often the ferrets will pile into one box to keep warm. Even in they do, be sure extra boxes are available.

It is useful if the shed arrangement contains one or more hutches, which need not be as substantial as those which are for outdoor use. These hutches may be needed to isolate a ferret for one reason or another. With

ferrets you will not have one problem that is often faced by those with rabbits or birds. Mice and rats will give the ferret home a wide birth—those foolish enough to enter the accommodation will not survive very long!

SAFETY PORCH

If an outdoor shed, with or without an enclosure attached to it, is to be erected it is wise to feature a safety porch in the design. This is simply a

Breeding groups of ferrets should be comprised of one color variety only.

small weldwired area you enter before going into the shed or enclosure. It removes the risk that should a ferret slip by you it cannot escape because it merely gains access to the safety porch. A final feature of any outdoor accommodation is that it should be fitted with a strong padlock. Unfortunately, whether you keep birds, rabbits, or even fish in a pond, there are those who may try to steal them. For added security it may be wise to also include a night light in the plans.

MULTI-BREEDING COURTS

The accommodation so far described in this text will prove very adequate for either

the pet ferret or a small breeding group comprizing only one color. However, should you wish to breed with ferrets of differing colors you will need to keep these separate, so that you have control over which ferrets mate with each other.

In such instances you can arrange the housing in much the same way as bird breeders arrange their aviaries. This is by having a row of shelters, which are the internal accommodations, opening to individual runs in which are kept the pairs or trios of each color variety. The shelter part should include a walkway for you to use as a service area. It will contain foods, bedding material, floor material, and the like, as well as good working surfaces.

Hopefully, the days are rapidly passing when ferret owners will regard the housing for their ferrets as being matters of no particular importance. If ferrets are to be kept they should receive as much consideration to their needs as any other animal. The accommodation should be well designed to be practical from your point of view, of very sturdy construction, and a place that the ferret will find comfortable. We owe them that much at least.

Do prepare the accommodation before you obtain the ferrets. This would seem an obvious statement, but you might be surprised how many people purchase ferrets and then rapidly nail a few planks together and place chicken wire mesh onto the front and then call this housing! If your ferrets are well housed they will be more content and make for better pets.

Ferrets are purchased for various reasons, and these will have some bearing on the way in which you go about the business of stock selection. In this book we are not concerned with those wanted as rabbiters, only those required as pets and breeding stock. We will discuss the pet ferret first, then look at the additional considerations a potential breeder must take into account.

SELECTING PET FERRETS

When you purchase any animal as a pet there is no guarantee just how good it will prove to be in this role. The factors that will determine this are many and interrelated. You can increase the odds in your favor by taking a sensible approach to the matter. The following are the various factors that you will need to consider.

HEALTH

This is the most important single factor when purchasing an animal for whatever reason it is required. In considering the health of the ferret you should commence by taking stock of the conditions the ferret is being kept under. If it is living in a dirty backyard shed this is not a good start. It is even worse if it is but one of many ferrets that are obviously overcrowded. Look at the state of the floor covering. If this is dirty, badly soiled with fecal matter, and smelly, the best thing to do is leave. This person clearly has no knowledge of how to look after ferrets, so is hardly likely to have quality stock suitable as pets.

Assuming you are satisfied as to the general cleanliness that the ferrets are being kept under, the next thing to do is to watch the ferrets as they move about. Are they all active, or are any not joining in with the others. Any that seem lethargic or totally disinterested in what is going on around them may be showing the first sign of an illness. If they are, there is a strong chance this will have been passed to the others, who will show the same clinical signs in a few days. Check that the youngsters all move without any impediment.

It may happen that the ferrets are all in a pile fast asleep, so it is a case of waiting until they are up and running about. Once you have selected one or two that seem lively and very interested in amusing themselves, and in watching you, it is time to go to the next stage.

Ask the seller to show you those you like. If the person

Ferrets can be warm and affectionate and even lick you like a dog. When you select a ferret as a pet be sure it is friendly.

seems rather cautious on this account it is usually because he or she is expecting to get bitten! This would indicate the ferrets have not been handled too frequently. In itself, it is not the end of the world, but is a point worthy of noting when it comes to comparing the stock with that of others you may see. The eyes of the ferret should be round and clear, with no signs of stained fur near them, or a discharge coming from them. The same is true of the nose, which should be just dry to damp, never running. The ears should be neat and erect. The fur should display no signs of bald patches, nor should any parasites be visible when you brush it against its lie with your hand. The anal region should be clean, with no signs of stained fur that might suggest a present or recent problem with diarrhea.

The belly will be smooth and soft, with no lumps or swellings. The feet will have five toes on each foot. If you are able to inspect the teeth these will be neatly aligned and white. The body will have substance. Although this is a slim animal this does not mean it is skinny, with bones obviously lacking a good covering of flesh. If the ferret has passed all of your inspections then, at that moment at least, it would seem to be a fine and fit example. More than this you cannot expect of the seller.

If they are prepared to guarantee the health for whatever period this is a bonus. Once in your possession the seller cannot know how the ferret will be looked after. A 14-day guarantee of health against major diseases

Young ferrets should be handled as often as possible. Many ferrets like to be petted.

is what you may be offered. If the ferret showed signs of these during this period it would indicate the animal was incubating the problem at the time you purchased it.

HOW MANY FERRETS TO PURCHASE

I would strongly recommend you purchase two ferrets as pets. These will provide company for each other when you are not around. They will also get into more mischief together, but this is part of the fun of owning them. They will give you much more pleasure in watching them play with each other, as well as with you. Further, the chances of your obtaining two ferrets with indifferent personalities is dramatically reduced.

WHICH SEX?

In terms of their personalities there really is no difference between hobs and jills. Either may prove to be more, or less, loving than the other. These are individual, not sex

related, traits. The hob will usually be larger than the jill, maybe even twice her size. This may be a consideration for you. He will be less expensive to desex, about half the price.

AGE TO PURCHASE

Ferrets are weaned from their mother when they are 6-8 weeks of age. The best time to obtain them is therefore at this stage. It is generally easier to tame them if they are very young. This does not mean that some older ferrets will not tame down as well, or even more so, than some youngsters. You should always be more cautious when purchasing the older ferret (such as an adult).

Unless it can be reasonably established via records, it is very difficult to determine the ferret's age once it is mature. The state of the teeth is the most reliable method, but this is subject to considerable variation depending on how the ferret has been looked after. The teeth of the older individual will be yellow, and the molars will have worn down more—but it would probably need a vet to inspect these to give an opinion.

Even if the ferret is a relatively young adult, and is easily handled, the owner may be selling it because it has developed some bad habits. Maybe it is not housetrained, or maybe it has got into the habit of ripping up the chair covers, because it was left for long periods on its own. Many of these psychological problems can be overcome—depending on how many chair covers you are prepared to have torn during the rehabilitation process!

Often, the adult is offered for sale by owners because it has become a biter through lack of correct management, or it has not been castrated, and they do not like its odor. Just now and then a really super pet becomes available because the owner's situation has changed, and they genuinely are not able to keep it, as much as they may want to. In their case they will be very concerned to know you are a loving owner. In the other cases they will be more con-

Ferrets are available in many colors but the colors are not indicative of their suitability as pets.

cerned to get rid of the ferret, so will not ask too many questions (if any) as to your suitability to care for the pet.

COLOR

There are a few color patterns that you can select from and these are discussed in the chapter on this subject. Here it can be stated that the color of a ferret is not in any way related to either its quality, or its suitability as a pet. This said, some comment is perhaps appropriate. The oldest established mutational color is the albino. For centuries breeders have preferred this as a working animal. Generally, the ferrets were selected on the basis of two features. One was their working ability, the other was their willingness to be handled. This has resulted in the fact that many people regard the albino as being less likely to bite, assuming it is well cared for and gently handled as a youngster. It is thus the selection for this feature that makes an albino less aggressive, not its color. Conversely, the albino's eyesight is generally held to be rather poorer than that of

full colored ferrets. This may make the albino more likely to nip at hands if it does not scent that they are the owners, or are not a food item. There are thus two opposing aspects involved.

I mention these facts for what they may be worth, and will add that in my experience color has no bearing on either the nature of a ferret, nor its eyesight. Far more important is the way it has been bred and reared. The color of the ferret may well affect its value. The albinos are the least expensive, while a well marked individual of any full color pattern is likely to command a better price.

VACCINATIONS

You are strongly advised to have your ferrets vaccinated against the major diseases that may be contracted by these animals. This may well have been done before you purchase the pet. If so, this will obviously increase the purchase price, but it is well worth the extra cost. Canine distemper, feline enteritis, rabies, and leptospirosis are among the more likely diseases that your vet will recommend protection against. The vaccinations may be given as early as 6 weeks, though 7-10 weeks would be more typical. Boosters may be given each year, or every second year, on your vet's advice.

CASTRATION AND DESCENTING

You are recommended to have hobs castrated and jills spayed in order to reduce both their natural body odors, and for other reasons. In the case of the hob it will make him less aggressive during the breeding season, and less desirous of wanting to escape in order to find a female. In the case of the jill it will remove the risk of problems in the event she is not mated. This aspect is discussed further in the breeding chapter.

It may be that the kits are already desexed when you obtain them, this being much more likely in the USA than in Great Britain, where it is usually not recommended to effect the surgery until the ferret is a few months old.

The descenting (removal of anal glands) of hobs is quite common in the USA, but less popular in Britain. It will further reduce the musky odor of the hob and can be done at the same time as castration, or later if you prefer. Discuss the matter with your vet because some may not be willing to remove anal glands on the grounds that it is mutilation for esthetic reasons only. There can be related problems when removing anal glands, so a vet may refuse to do this surgery on these grounds as well.

Your best place to buy a ferret is a pet shop or breeder who can show you at least three ferrets from which you can make a choice. Buy a ferret which has already been surgically treated (sexually neutered) and inoculated.

WHERE TO PURCHASE PET FERRETS

It is strongly recommended that you purchase a pet ferret from either a pet shop, or a breeder known to specialize in breeding pet ferrets. The former will no doubt have purchased stock from the latter. Both of these suppliers are more likely to offer castrated or spayed pets that have already been vaccinated and are ready to be taken home as pets. Further, they are both likely to have handled the youngsters on a regular basis to ensure they will not be a problem to the novice owner. The pet breeder will (or should) be engaged in a program that carefully selects as breeding stock only those adults that are easily handled, and are known to produce a high proportion of similar offspring.

Other potential sources, such as backyard breeders of inferior stock, or those who breed working ferrets, may not offer well handled youngsters, or ferrets that are fully treated as just detailed. Open markets are not suitable places to sell any animals from, so should be avoided.

THE MATTER OF CHARACTER

You should understand that all ferrets are very much individuals, so the way they react to being handled can vary considerably. For example, it would normally be assumed that a handreared ferret would make the best pet. This may indeed be so in 90% of cases, but that leaves the other 10% that may not.

We have handreared cats and ferrets only to find some turned out to be surprisingly indifferent to the fact that they should have been imprinted on humans. Likewise, an older ferret that has scarcely been handled at all can turn out to be very affectionate and gentle. You can never totally categorize any animal species, because one or two will always turn up that just do not follow the accepted patterns of behavior for their background.

This means that even a ferret from a very well proven line of gentle ferrets may prove to be the black sheep, even in a loving home. It's not that it may be unduly aggressive with you, but more likely that it will be less inclined to respond as might have been hoped. It may nip at times when most ferrets would not. This is why it is always best to have two pets, for you would indeed be unlucky to find both were of the very indepen-

Your selection of a ferret as breeding stock is not the same as selecting one for a pet. If breeding ferrets is your ultimate goal, start out with at least two ferrets (male and female) and learn about ferret breeding slowly.

dent types. If you have ever kept cats you will certainly appreciate how very different they can be, even though they have received exactly the same upbringing—but isn't this also true of children?

SELECTING BREEDING STOCK

The potential breeder of ferrets is advised to purchase a pair of pets before going out and obtaining breeding stock. In this way practical experience is gained in ferret management. Concurrent with this, you have the time to deliberate on whether ferret breeding really is what you want to do. You can also utilize the time in finding out many things that you will not know initially. Which are the most needed color varieties? What sort of breeding program will be used to improve quality? What sort of housing will be best for your needs?

If you are a beginner and attempt to make these decisions before you know anything about the hobby, the chances are you will have regrets at a later stage. It is much better to progress on a more low key basis, then move more seriously into the hobby as experience and knowledge has been gained and researched. The following aspects are the subjects that will be very important to you when you reach the stage of selecting breeding stock. Of course, many of the aspects already discussed will be as applicable to the breeder as they are to the pet owner. These are additional considerations.

STOCK OF KNOWN ANCESTRY

It is crucial that the serious ferret breeder has documented evidence of the initial stock's ancestry in terms of its genotype. If this is not

available wasted matings may have to be undertaken in order to find out about the purity of the line. For example, if you decide to breed any of the colored varieties, and knew nothing of their ancestry, you might be quite mystified if some albinos appeared in the first litter. For this to happen it would mean neither of the parents were pure for their color. Not a good start if you especially wanted to stick with one color variety. Likewise, if you saw in another breeder's establishment an outstanding albino in terms of its conformation, you might wish to know what colors the albino is masking. The owner could only tell you this if he or she knew from their breeding records.

Another aspect of ancestry is in relation to litter size and overall size of the offspring. These are under genetic influence, so you want to know that the stock you purchase comes from a line that is at least typical of the species for these aspects. Again, even motherhood is a genetic trait (which can be passed on via the hob as well), so you will clearly desire offspring from known good mothers.

It has already been stated in earlier text that docility is an inherited trait (though, like others, is subject to environmental influence) so you want stock from a line in which the breeder has made conscious selection for this trait. The only way any of these needs can be assessed is if the breeder has maintained accurate breeding records. Many do not, but in the ferret hobby of the future they will have to do if they wish to

The color of a ferret sometimes affects its selling price. Albino ferrets (shown above) are not always the same price as colored ferrets. Ferrets have many subtle color varieties (lower photo) which are only evident when you compare them side by side.

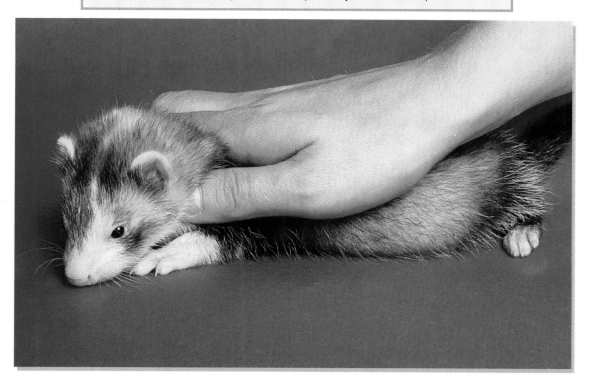

maintain a leading position in the hobby. It will not be enough to state that this or that is selected for unless documented evidence of this is available for scrutiny.

What must never be lost sight of is that a good looking ferret may be the result of pure random chance, or it may represent years of planned breeding—you want stock of the latter type. This does not mean you cannot commence your breeding operations with stock of unknown ancestry, but simply that life will be far easier if you have this information to begin with.

WHERE TO PURCHASE

It will be appreciated that the potential breeder really has only one possible source for breeding stock, and that is from an established breeder. No other source can hope to supply the background information that will be needed.

> **Your selection of a ferret should include a cursory examination of its health. Check its teeth but have the seller hold the ferret's mouth open for you to inspect. Don't try this with a ferret you don't know!**

There is another reason why a breeder is essential. This is in relation to the very possible need to purchase one or more examples of their breeding at a later date. It is very important that once breeding is underway the line of breeding starts to become purer—which can only happen if it is not crossed with stock whose ancestry is unknown.

You can breed nice ferrets on a very hit and miss system, but this is hardly serious breeding. You could find that after ten years your stock is no better than when you started! Most breeders try to improve the quality of their stock as the years go by, otherwise they are really doing nothing other than stock regeneration.

When initial breeding stock is being purchased it is wise to obtain this from a single source, not from two or more breeders. The logic is that if it comes from the same breeder there will be many common genes within each of the ferrets chosen. If you commence by mixing bloodlines (which are better termed gene lines) you will probably destroy the quality that each of the breeders has striven so

hard to create in their line.

Sometimes, however, a breeder will develop two quite distinct, though distantly related, lines in order that when an outcross is needed it is available without going beyond one's own stud.

INITIAL QUALITY

The potential breeder is wise to review as many breeder's lines as possible in order that a mental image is firmly established as to what constitutes quality in a ferret. At this time this is very much a matter of personal opinion, because there are no established written standards of excellence for ferrets. You will thus be part of the vanguard of the pet ferret hobby of the future, as it develops.

PRICE

The price of a ferret can vary dramatically from one source to another. Obviously, a backyard breeder who has devoted little time to quality breeding, or rearing hand tamed babies, is able to sell stock at a very low price. At the other end of the market the dedicated and caring breeder, with beautifully patterned and tame stock, will need to price this such that it reflects, at least in part, the time and effort placed into it.

Sometimes a casual breeder will actually give stock away just to get rid of it, but you are advised to support only those who meet the criteria. If the ferret has received vaccinations and surgery be prepared to pay the cost of these. Shop around when buying a ferret so you can assess what is the average cost of a pet or breeding animal of the standard you would like to obtain.

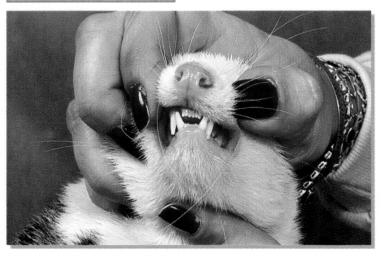

The ferret is a very easy pet to cater to in terms of its nutritional needs. As you meet other ferret owners you will no doubt receive a plethora of advice on what is the best regimen to adopt. In this chapter I will try to be as objective as possible, while relating the ways we feed our animals, and the philosophy behind it. You can then make up your own mind as to how you wish to feed your pets.

THE NEEDS OF CARNIVORES

Certain aspects of feeding are very flexible, such as when to feed, others are not. This includes what should and should not be included in the diet. The ferret is a prime carnivore and a secondary forager. This means its basic diet must be one of meat in various forms. Its digestive system evolved over millions of years to cope with meat—not vegetables. If you are a

vegetarian and attempted to make your ferret likewise you would be guilty of a cardinal error that would amount to cruelty. Your ferret would also be a very sickly and under-developed animal that would prove to be an extremely poor breeding specimen.

You may be able to change your diet, because the human is an omnivorous animal (evolved to eat food of animal and plant origin), but carnivores are not. They do not synthesize the gut bacteria essential to the breakdown of cellulose (and even you have to cook most vegetables before they can be utilized in your body). The microorganisms in the digestive tract of a carnivore are specialized to work on animal proteins. Vegetable matter is obtained in a partially digested state via the stomach of the ferret's prey—which are herbivores, meaning animals evolved to eat

plant matter. You should try to feed your ferret in harmony with the way it has evolved, not in total contradiction to this.

FEEDING UTENSILS

The best feeding dishes for ferrets are those made for cats or rabbits in crock. These are heavy, so not easily over-turned by the ferret, nor carried around or chewed on by enthusiastic youngsters. Try to obtain well glazed pots, as these will clean easier and last longer. Although you can supply water in similar dishes, the problem is that they soon become covered with a layer of dust, shavings, and other debris if they are placed in the cage.

It is therefore best to use automatic feeders, such as those made for rabbits. You want the models with aluminum tips that cannot be chewed by the kits. The bottles are suspended by wires to the ferret's cage. Check when purchasing your ferrets that the youngsters are familiar with these feeders. If they are not you should supply the water in a shallow dish, and fit a bottle feeder. Once the pets are seen to be using the bottle you can remove the open dishes. If the ferret is a pet that is given a lot of free roaming time in your home you can, as we do, supply the water, which is replenished daily, in an open dish.

If ferrets are kept out of doors it is essential that the water bottles are checked daily during cold weather. The tips can freeze, as can the water. The answer is to insulate the bottles, and warm the tips each morning—

The basis of a ferret's diet, the food from which he receives the most nutritional value, should be specially formulated ferret food. They are convenient and nutritionally balanced. Photo courtesy of 8 in 1.

or supply the water in an open dish during these periods.

WHEN & HOW OFTEN TO FEED

Exactly when you feed your ferrets is not important as long as it is to some sort of timetable. Your pets will become accustomed to this. We feed our pets on an ad lib basis throughout the day, supplying small amounts at each feeding. However, as I work from home this is no problem, but if you work at a place of business this system is obviously not possible—unless your wife or husband is at home during the day. I

state the polecat will not have unlimited access to food, some days it will feed well, others not at all. It is kept in shape both because of the restrictions on food availability, and by the fact it has to expend much energy in catching it. The pampered pet has neither of these problems to contend with. Assuming your time at home is limited, a sound regimen would be as follows. When you get up give the ferrets a meal (to be discussed later). You may then leave them a bowl of dried food to eat as they feel inclined. At lunchtime give

the family are out at work. However, if they are given a well balanced diet, and the correct amounts of this, they will survive well enough, and a whole lot better than millions did in bygone years.

HOW MUCH TO FEED?

There is no simple advice in reply to this question, because there are so many variables. The intake needs of a ferret will be affected by any or all of the following.

1. Age. Growing youngsters will consume more than an adult. They have to put on body weight, and replace the energy they burn up during playing—which ferrets do a lot of if they have the opportunity to do so. The adult's need will reflect its size and activity level. The older pet will eat somewhat less than it did when it was in the prime of its life.

2. Temperature. This embraces two areas of consideration. That of the time of the year, and that of the environment in which the ferret lives. Under natural conditions the polecat puts on a lot of weight during the autumn, because obtaining food in the winter becomes much more difficult. At this time the polecat needs the extra fat layers to provide insulation against the cold. During the peak of the summer it is able to subsist on a somewhat lower intake, because no food is needed to keep it warm. In the home environment the pet will normally never have a need to pile on the fat, because it will not need the same amount of insulation in the winter. If ferrets are kept outdoors they should receive more food in

should add that while frequent feedings are fine in many ways they are not without problems.

If any animal has an ad lib feeding regimen it will tend to become more fussy than if there is a reasonable lapse of time between meals during which it can build up an appetite. It may tend to become obese, so care must be exercised. In the natural

Many commercially offered ferret foods are enriched with vitamins, and vitamin supplements are available separately. Photo courtesy of Sun Seed Co.

them another small meal, with the main dinner in the evening. Kits really need 4-5 meals a day, but in the real world this is not always possible if both members of

Vitamins and minerals in syrup form can be licked from your finger...this is another bonding experience.

the autumn so they can develop the needed fat layers—they will become really chubby. The pet can be given a more regular sized diet throughout the year.

3. How Often to Feed. The amounts of food given at any one meal will reflect how many times per day the ferret is being fed. Its daily needs must be met across the number of times it is fed.

4. Quality of Food. The better the quality of food given, the less quantity will be needed. If a meal comprises a high percent of

throughout the nursing period than she would were she not breeding.

6. Convalescing. A ferret recovering from an illness will need more food, especially proteins, than it would normally eat. This is because while it was ill its food intake would have fallen dramatically. Its needs will have been obtained by oxidization of fat and muscle tissue, which must subsequently be replaced.

7. Metabolic Efficiency. Ferrets are just like other animals, including we hu-

does little but snooze most of the day! Likewise, an active pet will need more than one which is confined to a cage for long periods of the day.

Even allowing for all of the variables you may still be wondering how much food you should give to your ferrets. The yardstick is its health and condition. Place a given quantity down for it to eat. The ferret will only eat that which it needs. After two or three minutes it will show disinterest in any that might be left. If so, remove the dish and place it in the refrigerator (unless the quantity is so little that it may as well be trashed.)

If the ferret eats all that is given to it and is clearly seeking more, give it more until it is satiated. You now have an idea what it will eat at a single meal. At the second meal adjust the amount you supply up or down based on the first meal. Repeat the sequence at the third meal, and you now have a very good idea what it will consume in a day. It is very easy to establish normality by this trial and error method. That consumed will of course vary based on how much the ferret likes that day's menu, and on how it is feeling that day. Like us, ferrets have their good and bad days. If the ferret starts to become obese it is clearly being overfed, if it seems too thin it is not getting enough, or has some problem that will need veterinary advice. Never starve an overweight ferret. Instead, just reduce the size of its meals.

You may by all means leave some dry food down for the ferret to eat while you are out, and this will modify the

Now that ferrets are such popular pets, a tremendous amount of research has gone into their dietary requirements. It is important to feed your ferret a well-balanced and nutritious food that he will enjoy. You can find foods specifically formulated for ferrets at your local pet shop. Photo courtesy of Kaytee Products, Inc.

carbohydrate much more of this will be needed than if the percent of protein is high. Your pet can utilize the protein to build muscle—but not the carbohydrate, which is utilized as a fuel to provide muscular energy used in activity.

5. Breeding State. A breeding jill will consume a great deal more food just before and

mans. Some will become obese more quickly than others. Some survive on minimal intake, and are still very fit and handsome animals in the peak of condition. Others need a goodly amount of food in order to retain fitness.

8. Activity Level. A working ferret will consume much more food than a pet that

Modern color varieties sometimes change the mental outlook of the animal. This proud-looking animal commands a very high price for breeding purposes.

quantity of the food eaten at the three main meals. Some owners feed their ferrets mainly on dried concentrated foods, we prefer to supply a very wide ranging menu so that too much reliance is never placed on any one food type. This helps to avoid fussy eaters.

HOARDING

Ferrets, like hamsters, are natural hoarders of food. When they have finished a meal they may take uneaten scraps to some place they consider safe. This can be in a cupboard, in their sleeping quarters, or under an armchair cushion! They rarely eat this little cache, it being an instinctive habit derived from their wild polecat ancestors.

> Ferrets are like squirrels and hamsters. They hoard food. That is one reason why they should not be supplied with an excess of food.

They may eventually outgrow this habit, especially where mundane foods, such as dried chow, are concerned. However, rather than allow them to start hoarding, with the possible smells from decaying food, you can largely overcome any problems in one of two ways. If they are fed in the kitchen, which is recommended, remove uneaten food straight away. Alternatively, feed them in their cage, and check their sleeping quarters on a regular basis.

FOOD CONSTITUENTS

All foods are made up a number of constituents which are needed by animals in order to survive. You do not need to be an expert on these, but a fundamental knowledge of their role in nutrition is certainly useful in assessing the value of any given food item.

Proteins: These are found in foods of both plant and animal origins. Some essential proteins, however, are not found in plant foods. Foods of animal origin are by far the richest source of proteins. These substances are the building blocks of the body. When the ferret eats meat this is broken down by oxidization into its many amino acid constituents. These are then used to manufacture the needed proteins for muscle and other tissues. Of the total food intake of your ferret, about 30% of this should consist of proteins for the average adult. Youngsters, and breeding jills, need to have somewhat more, say 40%.

Popular sources of proteins are beef, poultry, selected white fish, cheese, eggs, milk, butter, meat extracts, and similar items. They must of course always be fresh. Offal, formerly very popular with ferreters, together with meats deemed unfit for human

consumption, should be avoided. They are rapidly colonized by bacteria, apart from being unpleasant to handle and difficult to store. Of the commercial canned, semi-moist, and dry foods, those produced for cats are superior to dog foods—which contain a higher percentage of cereals than is really good for a ferret.

An excess of proteins represents wasted food because it will either be converted to layers of fat, or will be burned up to provide energy. As protein foods are more expensive than other foods, you need to try and get the balance between these so you obtain maximum growth and condition, at the most economic cost.

Fats: The main role of these foods in the body are that they are the most efficient sources of energy (twice that of proteins and carbohydrates), are essential for the transportation of fat soluble vitamins around the body, and they give food its taste. Low fat diets will be less acceptable than those with a somewhat higher fat content. Few studies on the fat needs of ferrets have been made, but it is assumed that a content of about 20-30% of the diet should be fat in its various forms. This is based on studies in cats and rats.

Sources of fat are much the same as those for proteins, with fish oils being totally fatty in make up. Butter and lard are also nearly 100% fat in content. A lack of fat in the diet will result in poor fur growth, scaly skin, lack of potential size growth, and an increased susceptibility to illness. However, excess fat

will result in obesity, poor utilization of vitamins, and lethargy, so moderation is the key word, as it usually is in all aspects of animal nutrition.

Carbohydrates: These provide the most readily available form of energy to any animal species. They are made essentially of sugars. All plants contain these constituents, but the richest sources are grain crops, such as wheat, barley, maize, rice and their by-products, such as breakfast cereals, cookies, dog biscuits and bread. Ferrets, along with most other carnivores, actually have no proven need of these ingredients directly in the diet. This is because their constituents can be synthesized by the breakdown of proteins and fats. They are included in the diet of most carnivores because they provide bulk to the menu, and are inexpensive. Generally, about 40% of the total food intake of a pet ferret will be in the form of carbohydrates, via their byproducts, which are more easily assimilated into the body.

Vitamins: These are not actually foods in themselves, but are essential to the absorption of foods, and the prevention of illnesses. Without vitamins your ferret would die. They are found in all foods, but the richest sources are fruits, together with the liver of animals. Many are stored in the latter organs, which is why they are such a rich source. If your ferret is given a well rounded diet it will not be deficient of any vitamins, so the need for supplements will not be required. Indeed, excess vitamins will prove to be as

dangerous to the ferret's health as a lack of them.

Minerals: These are elements, such as calcium, iron, copper, sulfur, potassium, iodine, magnesium and many others. They are generally required in trace amounts, though calcium, phosphorus and magnesium are needed in somewhat higher concentrations, though even these are only needed in very small amounts in relative terms. It is most unlikely that your ferret would ever suffer from a general mineral shortage. More likely is either a calcium deficiency, or an excess of this, both states being undesirable. The pregnant and nursing jill has an increased calcium need for the strong bone and teeth development of her kits—and to replace her own levels which fall as she suckles the young on her milk.

Water: This precious food is often underrated by novices. An animal can survive longer without food than it can without water. It should always be available to your ferret. The amount consumed will reflect the diet. Pets fed an a basically dry diet will drink much more than those which receive moist foods. In some localities the water authorities put so many chemicals into the drinking water, to kill bacteria, that it becomes unappealing to animals—who will drink from puddles rather than from faucet water. A water purifier fitted to the system may be as much to your own benefit as to that of your pets.

FEEDING COMMENTS
When planning the feeding regimen of your ferrets try to

make this both interesting for them, yet well balanced in its constituents. A good base to the diet will be various foods made specifically for ferrets. These are very convenient and are fortified with vitamins after the cooking process in order to replace water soluble vitamins destroyed by cooking. Both canned (moist) and dry ferret foods are on the market, so you can choose which ever you prefer. Each type has own advantages.

Cooked vegetables can be mixed in with the regular foods, but bear in mind that ferrets invariably do not like much vegetable matter, so only add a few bits and see which are taken. The same is true of fruits.

Meat can be offered in both cooked and raw form. Raw meat must of course be fresh. If taken from the refrigerator, ensure it has fully thawed. Raw meat is excellent for the teeth and jaw muscles. Liver, kidney, spleen and other organs can be given in small quantities and are useful foods, especially liver. Eggs can be given raw (much relished, but rather messy) or hard boiled. Do not give more than one or two in a week. White fish is fine, but give herring, mullet and their like only in moderation as they contain thiaminase which can restrict thiamine content in the body. This is very important to ferrets (and cats, dogs and other pets).

Bread and milk, or cereals and milk, are old ferret keeper favorites, but are not really good as regular dietary items. Too much, milk will result in the ferrets

having diarrhea. Give them some low fat milk, or evaporated milk which has been diluted with water. Milk in the form of ice or whipped cream will be eaten with enthusiasm—but give it only in a small amount as an occasional treat.

Do not feed sweet items, such as candies, to your ferrets. Hard bones, real or artificial, are fine for your pets. They will keep them busy for some time if they have a little meat on them, and will help clean their teeth, as well as provide

When planning your ferret's diet be sure to include some variation to keep it interesting for him. An occasional well-placed snack will help keep your ferret excited about mealtime. Photo courtesy of Sun Seed Company.

We all love our pets and want to treat them to something special occasionally. Sweet items, such as candy, can be dangerous to your ferret. Instead feed him nutritious, specially formulated snacks available at your local pet shop. Photo courtesy of 8 in 1.

good jaw exercise.

As with all matters of husbandry you should take in all the advice that is given to you, think about it, and utilize that which you feel is best for your pets. At the end of the day, the general health and activity level of

your ferrets will be the ultimate guide as to whether or not you are giving them a sound diet. If their eyes are bright, their bodies muscular, their fur sleek, and their droppings firm and dark, this means their diet is sound.

DIETARY PROBLEMS

If you feel that the condition of your ferrets is not what you think it should be when compared to other ferrets, seek the advice of your veterinarian. If a ferret has a nutritional imbalance you need to know exactly what the cause is before trying to remedy the problem. Only a vet has any hopes of diagnosing the problem and suggesting a remedial course of action.

You can feed your ferret natural hard bones, or an even safer chew device are the Nylabones® made for dogs. Those Nylabones which are liver flavored are best. Hard Oodles™ made of carrots, are bone-hard chews which are sold for hamsters but are perfect for ferrets.

Once you have prepared the accommodation and have selected a nice youngster (but two are better), you should try and collect your pet as early in the day as possible. Take a strong cardboard box filled with hay in which it can be transported home. Make some air holes in the box. Check with the seller what the ferret has been fed and purchase a small quantity of the food. Even though you may wish to widen the diet supplied, it is best to stick with what it has been having for the first few days.

At this time it will be a little stressed, so you do not want to add to this by offering it foods it is not familiar with. Do remember that as you begin to include new items into the diet this should always be done on a gradual basis, otherwise the result will probably be an upset stomach and diarrhea.

Once home, the pet can be placed straight into its cage so it can become familiar with this. After it has had time to inspect the cage, offer it a small meal, then leave it alone to settle down and have a sleep. If you have young children, instruct them not to disturb the ferret and not to place their fingers into the cage.

HANDLING A FERRET

If you have heeded the advice in the chapter on stock selection, your new pet will be one that has already been handled a great deal from the time it first left the nest. This will not be a new experience for it, but it still needs to get to know you. Once it has had a nap, woke up, and eaten a small meal, you can then take it out of its cage. Before doing this talk soothingly to it.

As with any animal it is important that it knows what your intentions are. You should not suddenly grab at it. Rather, let it see your hand, because it is important that it associates this only with nice things—such as being picked up gently and being handed tidbits. If you are unsure how it will react to you the best thing to do is to place your clenched index finger to its mouth so it can sniff it. If it attempts to nip, do not snatch the finger away, but push it forward into its mouth.

If this is done a few times it will go off the idea of nipping the finger. The bite of a baby is exploratory, so is not comparable to that of a ferret biting in earnest, which would be very painful. If your pet simply sniffs or licks your finger you can see if it will let you stroke it. If so, do this, then in a smooth single action place your hand around its shoulders, with your thumb under its jaw, and your other fingers passing under its chest. In this way you can hold it securely as well as restrict its ability to nip you. Lift it up and support its rear legs with your other hand.

> The best way to test the friendliness of a ferret is to offer him your clenched finger! It takes bravery but don't pull your finger away if the ferret chomps on it.

You can now sit down and, resting its rear legs on your body, stroke it gently and talk to it, while still retaining a hold on its shoulders. If it seems quite happy you can let go of it and let it explore your lap. Once it is familiar with you it can be picked up simply by placing your hand under its chest, much in the manner you would pick up a puppy.

As stated earlier in this book, a ferret is only a suitable pet for adults and children who are old enough to be instructed in the correct handling of these animals. A toddler should never be allowed to handle a ferret because such children can hold them too hard—and the ferret may bite as a result. Some ferrets are really placid and would not bite even a toddler, but you cannot be sure of this, so it is best to play safe.

As with all pets, the secret to success in owning a placid ferret is to handle it often and gently. It must be picked up a great deal during the first few days it joins your household, and you should talk to it a great deal. Give it a name and it will come to this—if it feels like it. Remember, a ferret is not like a dog that will come on command—compare it always with a cat.

It may seem that in this, and any other book on ferrets, that the aspect of nipping comes up a great deal. This is not because the ferret is any more aggressive than a cat, dog, or parrot, but because its teeth are sharp, and its reactions very fast. When it is a baby it gets used to biting its littermates, and anything else. This stage may have largely passed by the time you

obtain if from the seller, or it may still be doing this and needs to learn what it can and cannot do.

You can give a youngster a tap on the flanks if it gets too excited when playing with you. But any discipline must be at the moment of an act, never afterwards, otherwise the pet will not associate the spank with the action. Do not spank your pet on the head, only on the flanks, and only hard enough for it to get the message. Ferrets are intelligent animals and learn quickly if taught in a consistent manner.

HOUSE FREEDOM

Before allowing your pet ferret the total freedom of your house, you should carefully check it out, room by room, for any likely avenues of escape. These will be holes in floor boards, or in the skirting woodwork. Ferrets can get through surprisingly small holes, so see these are blocked. It is also wise to consider what things may be

> If a ferret comes to you it is probably more friendly than if it goes away from you.

a potential danger to an inquisitive ferret. These would include electric heaters on which it might burn itself if it placed its paws on the front guard rails.

Any shelves that the ferret can get on it certainly will in order to explore them. Apart from knocking things over that might fall on it, there is the obvious risk it could damage valued ornaments and their like—so see that these are placed in a safe position. In a kitchen there are many dangers, such as ceramic heating hobs, trailing wires from an electric iron, and hot pans on stoves. If it is washing day, always double check that the washing machine, or the tumble dryer, does not contain a ferret having a nap! Finally, always be sure no outside doors or low windows are open when the ferrets are loose.

GROOMING

Pet ferrets should be groomed on a very regular basis. This serves a few useful purposes. It means you are handling the ferret a lot, which is a good thing. It keeps the fur and skin in good health, and it enables you to routinely give it a physical check over. The grooming can be done with any semi-stiff handbrush and a medium toothed comb. Use the brush first to remove any tags or debris, then run the comb through the hair. If grooming is commenced with a youngster it will come to accept this— whether or not it enjoys it will depend on how gentle you are. If you hurt your pet do not be surprised if it attempts to do likewise to you!

Bathing is not normally necessary, but some owners like to attend to this in order to remove any trace body odors. The water should be just warm, never too hot. Groom the ferret first so there is no risk of tangles becoming mats. Be very sure no water enters either the ferret's eyes or ears. A mild baby shampoo, or one produced for cats, will be fine. Soak the ferret first, then rub in the shampoo. Rinse the shampoo out very thoroughly, otherwise it will dry in the coat and may set up an irritation, as well as leave the coat with a lack of luster.

Dry the fur by giving it a brisk toweling. A hair dryer can also be used, but take great care that the nozzle is never placed too near the skin—with the attendant risk of burning the ferret. This would really put it off being bathed and dried. During the grooming process you can carefully check your pet's fur for parasites, as well as the state of its teeth and ears. Check the paws to see they have no abrasions or thorns between the pads.

LEAD TRAINING

Ferrets can be trained to walk on a lead much as a dog

Your local pet shop will offer harnesses made especially for ferrets, rabbits and other small mammals.

can. They accept this more readily than most cats will. It is best to use a cat harness on your ferret rather than a collar, because it can easily slip the latter should it become startled or frightened. Be very sure it is a snug—not overtight or loose—fit. Let it become used to wearing the harness before you attach a lead to it. The lead can then be attached and you can practice walking with your pet in a quiet place, such as your garage or garden.

Let it explore as it wants to, but then gently pull on the lead and call the ferret, to encourage it to go in the direction you wish to. Never drag it along. Walking on a lead should be done in stages, a few minutes per lesson, so it does not get boring. You can take your pet into the local park or the countryside but never allow it off the lead, and always pick it up if you see a dog approaching. When out walking you will find that a ferret is a real eye catcher to most people, who will want to talk to you about your strange looking pet.

When in the yard you can attend to your chores while the ferret can be given reasonable freedom on the end of a line attached to a peg secured in the ground. Of course, if your yard is not completely fenced you must take care that dogs do not come around when they see this unusual animal on the lawn—cats normally will not bother a ferret.

PLAYING

When ferrets are introduced to others of their kind owned by fellow enthusiasts, they usually take to each other straight away. In this they differ from cats. They will often quickly start to play with each other, especially if they have been neutered. In the home you will find them very playful. If they have some cardboard tubes and boxes, rubber balls, cotton reel bobbins and similar items, these will amuse them for hours. They will also find lots to do if you are sorting through your cupboard drawers. They will want to get in and have a good look at everything, because there is sure to be something to play with in such places.

They greatly enjoy being stroked and tickled and will roll over on your lap so you can do this to them. If you do this very gently they usually fall asleep while on their backs. When playing with their own kind they will dash about all over the place chasing each other and wrestling. Like cats and dogs, they will also chase imaginary prey, as well as arching their backs and raising their fur as they run sideways.

With other house pets, such as dogs and cats, they will also enjoy playing once each knows the other. Ferrets are very much touch players, by which I mean they enjoy a rough and tumble, as do dogs. Cats, on the other hand, prefer to chase without actually wrestling (other than when they are kittens). They will thus invariably find a good vantage point above the ferret where they can bop it on the head with their paws as it tries to reach them.

All in all you will find the ferret is a truly delightful pet that, along with such critters as the skunk, is nothing like the animal of its reputation. Ferrets are extremely affectionate: if you spend enough time with them, they will follow you all over the house and want to be with you all the time. Chances are that if you only obtain one, you will soon be wanting a companion for him—if you have two, you will probably soon have three or four.

Above: Ferrets are very playful and love toys...but be sure the toys are strong, as ferrets love to chew. Below: Some ferret varieties have white feet and some brown feet. Ferrets love to nap with another friendly ferret.

Once you have gained experience as a ferret owner you may start to think in terms of becoming a breeder. This is not a step that should be undertaken without a great deal of thought. There are probably more negatives to this than there are advantages. The average enthusiast is far better to stick to pets and really enjoy these. However, if you do wish to consider the possibility of becoming a breeder let us look at both sides of the coin.

THE DISADVANTAGES OF BREEDING

The first thing that can be said about breeding ferrets is that it will definitely not make you any money. If this was one of the reasons the idea appealed to you, forget it. Even commercial fitch farms struggle to make it pay. The high time investment into breeding pet quality ferrets is such that the best you can hope for is that the sale of surplus stock will defray some of your overheads in being able to do something you really find enjoyable. Like most hobby pursuits, all of the talk you hear of making money from them rarely ever proves true, that is, assuming you are caring for the pets as you should.

A litter of young kits can be very demanding in both time and cost terms. There is the additional food bill, the cost of vaccinations and other veterinary bills, plus the extra caging and accommodation needed. You then need to advertise the kits, and will have a succession of people coming to see them—some of whom may not appeal to you at all as possible owners of your stock. Others are simply time wasters. Casual breeding offers little benefit, which means you need to think in terms of developing a small stud—which increases the time, accommodation and other costs.

These three ferrets are of three different color varieties. Decide which color you want to breed and don't experiment with inbreeding the various color varieties.

ADVANTAGES OF BREEDING

The singular benefit of breeding most pet animal species comes from the personal inner satisfaction this provides in seeing babies born and grow into beautiful adults. The serious breeder enjoys planning the matings, the challenge of trying to improve the quality of the stock, or its colors. Simply being able to own a larger collection of ferrets is sufficient fulfillment to most breeders.

Breeding creates a need for larger accommodations, and even this provides satisfaction to many people. They may enjoy planning this all out, and seeing the ideas come to fruition. It is comparable to those whose hobby may be a garden pond and its immediate surroundings, or the aviculturist developing a range of esthetically pleasing aviaries. Breeders also enjoy meeting other breeders to compare ideas and stock—so there is a social aspect to it as well.

Ultimately, for the pet ferret breeder, there is the satisfaction that comes from helping to establish the ferret as a leading pet, and taming the babies, which are always a constant source of pleasure—as well as of a worry. As the hobby gains in stature the present day breeders will become the stalwarts of the future; no doubt a select few of these will be able to make ferret breeding a paying hobby, as has happened in cats, dogs, koi, budgerigars and other pets. If you carefully consider the implications of breeding, and still feel sure you wish to become more deeply involved in the hobby, the rest of this chapter will give you a good idea of how to go about this.

The soft sable look with dark feet is currently one of the most popular varieties, therefore making it the most expensive.

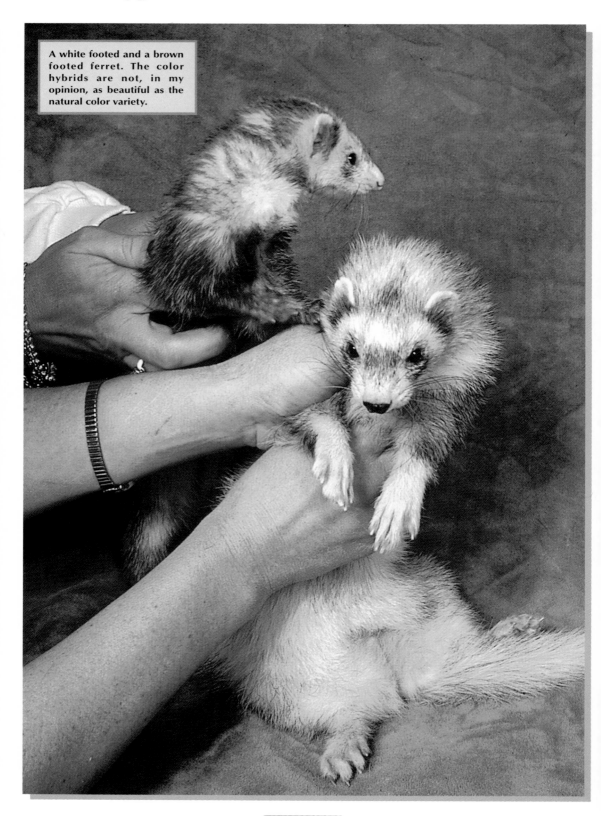

A white footed and a brown footed ferret. The color hybrids are not, in my opinion, as beautiful as the natural color variety.

PLANNING

Aspects that will need planning will be in relation to the extra accommodations needed, the day to day management time of the stock, and of course obtaining suitable ferrets to form the foundation of your stud. These subjects have all been discussed in earlier chapters. Commit you ideas to paper, try to join a ferret club, and try to visit other breeders so you can gain from their ideas. They will be delighted to discuss those things that have proved successful, as well as the problems and disasters they may have experienced over the years.

BREEDING AGE

A ferret may attain sexual puberty as young as five months of age, and a jill may be capable of breeding at this age. However, this is best avoided, as breeding with any very young female has only disadvantages. If she is bred from before she is fully mature this will result in her failing to attain her potential growth size. It may also result in the offspring being less vigorous than would otherwise be the case. With a very young male the problems are not so significant, because as long as he is capable of producing fertile sperms his physical state will be largely unaffected by the act of mating.

It is advisable, other than with two mature ferrets, to always mate a maiden jill with an experienced hob, or vice versa. Apart from the obvious advantages of pairing an experienced animal with one that is previously unmated, there is the fact that if a litter is not forthcoming it narrows down the possibility of an infertile specimen to the unproven one of a pair.

BREEDING CONDITION

There are two aspects to this term. One is related to the actual reproductive state of the ferrets, the other to the general health of the ferrets, irrespective of whether they are sexually in a breeding state. Regarding general health, never attempt to breed from a ferret that is obese, especially a female. This dramatically increases the risk of problems being created by the excess weight and fat on the individual.

Ensure both prospective partners are in really hard condition. This state is reached by their having ample room in which to exercise. Many failed matings in all pets species are directly caused by a lack of condition, because the breeder attempts to keep too many individuals, thus restricts them to limited accommodations in a breeding room. The actual reproductive state of readiness in ferrets is seasonal in the wild, but may not be under conditions of artificial lighting. This is because in the wild the ferret is a photoreceptive breeder. This means that both sexes come into a breeding state depending on the length or intensity of daylight hours and wavelengths. They perceive the increased, or reduced, intensity of daylight, and this triggers physical changes in their bodies.

The male reacts to reduced light hours, when his testes descend into the scrotal sacs and produce spermatazoas—the means of inheritance. This begins to happen in December, so that by late February he is able to produce sperms, his testes now being very visible. He will remain in a breeding state for about five months, until the end of July, after which his testes move back into his body cavity. Thus, in August through September his fertility is less reliable. From October until February he is not interested in, and may be incapable of, successful mating. It is thus a gradual process. At the beginning and end of the breeding season he may well mount the female, but may not be able to produce fertile sperms. The female pituitary glands respond to increasing hours of daylight before they trigger the steady growth of the female's vulva, and the production of fertile eggs. The process begins in mid February. Once underway the jill is said to be in estrus, and she will remain in this state until mated, or until the end of her breeding period, which is also about August. Once mated, irrespective of whether or not this is a fertile mating, her vulva will start to decrease in size some days after the mating has taken place. She will also refuse the advances of any males.

The peak breeding period is usually between April and May, when both sexes are, at least in theory, at the height of their sexual states. In reality, this can vary such that a male may be late or early in coming into a breeding state, as could the female.

SEXUALLY READY ADULTS

To complete your background knowledge of reproductive sexuality in ferrets we should consider the consequences of owning ferrets capable of breeding (sexually entire), but not allowing them to. In the case of the male, he will be much more aggressive once in breeding condition. He will also carry a stronger than normal scent, and will urinate around the home. He will go through his mating routine with any females, even though they may have been spayed. This entails biting them on the neck, and generally giving them a rough time.

For the average breeder it is probably better not to own an entire male, but to use the services of a stud ferret when this is needed. This is quite normal in horses and cats, which are other pets in which the entire males can be a problem to the average breeder conducting only a restricted breeding program.

With a nonbreeding, but unaltered, female the problems are much more serious. Once in estrus, with a fully enlarged vulva, she remains this way as already stated until mated, or until the breeding season is over. If it is not intended to breed from her, and nothing is done to terminate the estrus, she will be at considerable risk of contracting a uterine infection, from which she will probably die. This is because her swollen vulva is a prime site for bacterial colonization. The longer she remains in a breeding state, the greater the chances of infection. For these reasons the pet female should be spayed, and the male castrated.

If it is intended to skip a breeding season with one of your jills, she should either receive hormonal injections by your vet to bring her out of estrus, or she should be mated to a vasectomized hob. The vasectomized hob can go through the full mating routine, but cannot pass sperms to the jill. The female will then have a pseudopregnancy, go out of estrus, and react as though she was pregnant. Such jill's can make excellent auntie ferrets for others who may have large litters to cope with.

ARTIFICIAL LIGHTING

Under normal conditions, wild polecats may rarely breed twice during the season, but the ferret may be induced to breed three or four times in a season under conditions of artificial daylight. This means that the breeding season becomes year round, as is possible in birds and many other pets when artificial daylight is created by using fluorescent or other lighting. There is nothing to be gained from this practice—other than more offspring. It is this reason that prompts many breeders to become involved in such breeding strategy. They are more concerned about themselves, and the extra cash they might gain, than they are about the animals they keep.

The negatives of year round breeding are that it dramatically reduces the vigor of the female, and ultimately of her offspring. Her useful breeding life will be reduced, indeed, her life expectancy itself may be shortened. As it is not the objective with any pet to propagate the species for commercial gain, as in chicken or beef production, there is no reason why the hobbyist should try to maximize on the potential number of litters produced. When you breed for quality you should restrict the number of litters of your ferrets to just one, at the most two, per season, only if there is special need for this, and if the female is vigorous.

THE MATING

Once the female's vulva has swollen to its full extent, which is about 7-10 days after you first notice a swelling, she will be ready to be bred from. When introduced to the male he will scent her condition and, assuming he is in a breeding state, will start to chase her around. She will not allow him to mate her until she is ready, but after some time she will go limp and let him mount her. He will grab her by the neck in what at times can seem a very violent manner, rather like the situation in cats. He may drag her about and throw her from one side to the other, but do not intervene, this is normal ferret love-making! Eventually copulation will take place. The actual time a tie takes (the period when the two are locked together) can vary from a only a few minutes to maybe two or more hours.

Once a mating has taken place the jill can be removed, or she can be left with the hob for 24 hours, in which case more matings, and more rough treatment, will ensue.

PREGNANCY

The jill can be treated just as normal after being mated. She should be given the same exercise facility and the same diet. The diet can be altered progressively with each week of the pregnancy, by giving her rather more food, proteins in particular, and maybe milk soaked into bread. Whether or not the mating was successful will not be evident until about the 21st day after the mating. At this time your vet may be able to feel the kits by palpitation. Even this may not be possible, for it has happened more than once that a jill has had a quite large litter without her abdomen being distended, as you would normally expect to happen.

The gestation period (the time between the fertilization of eggs and the birth of the kits) is normally about 42 days or six weeks. About the third or fourth week into the pregnancy you should provide the jill with a good nesting box, if she does not already have one. It should contain at least three inches of lining material, such as clean wood shavings, and an ample supply of quality straw (not hay, which will create too much heat). You can also supply some dry leaves which she may utilize as part of the nest lining. If she has been sharing accommodations with other jills it is time to remove her, or the other jills, because she will become increasingly less tolerant of these.

If you are breeding with a jill in the household it would be wise to commence placing her in her cage or living quarters for progressively longer periods each day after about the fourth week. This is so that by the time the litter is born she will be spending most of her time in the cage, and will not be seeking some quiet spot in your house to have the litter.

THE BIRTH

In most instances the ferret will give birth to her litter without any problems. The first you may know of the exciting event is when you hear the kits squealing. There are two trains of thought with regard to the birth process, so I will relate each in order that you can make your own decisions, taking all factors into account.

1. Some breeders will not interfere at all with a jill that has given birth to a litter. If there are problems these are left to run their course. The theory is that by leaving the jill to herself the stress factor is totally removed and a natural situation prevails. Any jill that is unable to produce and rear her litters is of little value to any breeding program. By interfering, which may only mean trying to see how things are going, a person may unwittingly trigger off a defense mechanism in even the friendliest of ferrets, especially a first time mother. The problems will be discussed shortly.

2. Some breeders carefully monitor all stages of the birth in order that they are able to render assistance if this is needed. If they do not monitor the situation, they are in no position to offer help. They believe that by this approach many kits that might otherwise have died can be saved. Further, once the kits are born, only by monitoring their progress (such as by weighing them every other day) can problems be detected in order that a remedial course of action can be put underway.

The benefits and negatives of both views should be respected because, in ferrets,

as in most other forms of livestock, there is ample evidence to support both views. Whole litters have been lost due to breeder interference—but the young of many rare species of animals have been saved due to breeders stepping in when things were clearly not going well.

BIRTH PROBLEMS

It should be stressed that in the majority of cases the birth of litters will present no problems. Even so, the breeder should be aware of what can go wrong, and what might be done to try and resolve the situation. A maiden jill can become frightened by her own babies as they are born. She may devour one or all of them. Alternatively, she may go to the litter pan to give birth to them, or elsewhere if she is free roaming in the home. This is why it is not a good idea to let her roam free when a litter is imminent—you may not find one or more of the babies until it is too late. This nervous reaction to her own offspring may be a natural one, or it may have been induced (in the case of her eating her babies) by breeder interference, or by some other situation that made her feel insecure. An example would be a barking dog in close proximity to her accommodation, or other people, or machinery nearby.

Sometimes the jill will react quite correctly after the first baby is born, while with others the first litter may not survive, but subsequent ones are cared for as they should be. Should a jill prove to be a bad mother on two occasions, it would be wise not to use her again for breeding. In certain species of birds, such as Gouldian finches, it has become the normal situation to remove chicks and foster them to other species, because the hens are such poor mothers. Never foster out ferret kits for this reason, otherwise you create the same situation. Motherhood is under genetic influence, so poor mothers should be spayed and kept only as pets. This said, you should also check back through the father's line to see if the trait may have come from his mother, and been passed by him to his daughters.

If babies are born in the litter tray you can gently place them back into the nest box, or transfer them to a foster mother if one is available. Another jill who is about to give birth will normally accept such babies, as will a mother with a recently born litter. When making the decision as to which course of action should be taken you will have to take into account what you know about the character of the natural mother. Another problem that may happen is that when the kits are born the mother may not wash any residual amniotic membrane from the face of the kits. If this is not done the kits will suffocate. You can gently tear the membrane, or wipe it away with a damp cloth. Shortly, the baby will take a gasp of air and start to cry, when all is normally well. Likewise, if the jill fails to bite through the cord that served as a life line from the kit to its placenta, this could strangle the kit. It should be severed a short distance from the navel. A small amount of blood will

be extruded, after which it should dry and will shrivel up.

A jill may fail to nurse her kits either due to reasons already discussed, or because she has no milk. In either case the kits will need a foster mother. The babies may not feed from the mother for a few hours, but should do so at this time in order to receive the vital antibodies in the initial milk that will give them protection against infections.

REARING THE KITS

The number of kittens your ferret may have is very variable, ranging from 1-19. The average will be in the order of 5-8. These will be born at intervals of a few minutes, but this again is very variable, and there can be delays of a few hours between some births, especially with a nervous jill. The last kitten may appear as late as a day after the rest of the litter are born. If, after this time, the jill appears unsettled and distressed you should immediately seek veterinary advice, because there may be an offspring still trapped in the womb for one reason or another.

The kits are born blind and deaf. They appear naked, but actually do have a fine coat of fur that becomes apparent once they have dried out. For the first couple days the mother will remain with the kittens, leaving her nestbox only to use her litter tray. Thereafter, she will leave the nest to feed as well. Regardless of the ultimate color of the kits, they will all be white at first, the color starting to form after about ten days. The albino is evident even when its eyes are sealed, because these will be pink, whereas a

colored ferret will display a darker area behind the eyelids.

As the kits reach the two week mark they are able to scramble about. If it is possible for them to clamber out of their nestbox they will do so with mother continually having to carry them back. Although they are still unable to see, they can smell food and will move towards this. By three weeks of age they can cope with soft foods, such as canned cat food on which powdered milk can be sprinkled. This can be placed into the nest and will take some of the strain from the mother. Large litters are always a problem to the jill because she has only eight nipples, so there is always a demand from her kits. At three weeks of age the teeth of the babies are very sharp, and can in fact cope with soft solid foods. It will be appreciated that young ferrets, like other infants, are very messy eaters, so you will probably need to start wiping them at this age. Over the next couple of weeks the eyes of the youngsters will be fully open, and they will also be getting around very well. They are very playful at this age and will test their mother's patience to the limit. They can be given minced meats as well as milk at this age as they are now almost ready to be weaned.

The mother will have lost a great deal of weight, and her continually having to drag the kits back into the nest becomes more of a strain on her—for they are getting heavier by the day. Sometimes a female friend of the jill can be used as an auntie, and this really does help the mother to cope with the

youngsters. However, some jills will not tolerate other females near her babies, so it's a case of experimenting to get to know the various characteristics of your stock.

WEANING

The kits are weaned when about 5-8 weeks of age. In order that this process goes smoothly, and for the psychological as well as the physical well being of the jill, it should be done gradually. Remove the most well developed kits first, then take the others one or two at a time every few days. They can be placed in nursery accommodation. By this method the jill's milk will dry up gradually, and she will

ensuring that the accommodation of the ferrets never gets too hot. This can cause many complications. Be very sure fresh water is always available to the jill when she is pregnant and rearing offspring, as any deficiency in liquid intake will almost certainly have disastrous results.

HANDLING POTENTIAL PET YOUNGSTERS

While some breeders handle their kits almost from the time they are born, others wait until the kits first scramble out of the nest at 2-3 weeks of age. At this time, although they are still blind, they are extremely receptive to environmental conditions, so it is an

COLONY BREEDING

Ferrets can be bred on a colony system which comprises of a number of jills, castrated hobs, and variously aged offspring. However, such a system can result in problems until a workable family unit is established. It does require that the ferrets have plenty of room, and that there are more than enough nestboxes for the jills. The presence of unaltered males is risky to such a colony, but some have been kept within the commune without problem. The castrated hob, however, may prove to be a very good uncle to the kits, as is often the case in cats.

In this chapter the bare

not have the trauma of finding her kittens suddenly taken from her. As much of a drain as they have been on her, she is still a mother with all that this implies with regards to her offspring.

At weaning age the kittens should be receiving a well balanced adult diet. The difference is that the size of pieces of meat given to them will reflect their small size. Throughout the rearing period you can greatly reduce the chances of problems by

ideal time to start handling and talking to them. Indeed, it will determine to a very large degree how well they become imprinted on humans.

Regular handling from this time onwards should ensure that by the ideal time they leave their litter mates, at 7-10 weeks, they will be very tame and have no fear of humans. As a breeder, it is your responsibility to ensure they are well reared, well handled, and in the best possible state to go to a new home.

> **The female ferret gets heavier as she gets closer to giving birth. The female will deliver about six weeks after a successful mating.**

bones of breeding have been discussed. The potential breeder is therefore recommended to obtain more specialized works that deal with complications, handrearing, and other aspects of the subject that the enthusiastic breeder should know about.

This chapter is divided into two interest areas. The first will be informative to both the pet owner and the breeder. The second will be of particular interest to breeders, though the pet owner may wish to learn something about the subject in order to broaden their knowledge.

FERRET COLORS

Compared to most other popular pets, the range of available colors and patterns seen in the ferret is very limited. This reflects the fact that this species is comparatively new in terms of breeder interest in color varieties. The ferreter of old largely favored the albino, so there was no compelling desire to try and develop colors. The fitch farmer has more interest in color, but as the skins of the ferret can be dyed, even this group of owners has not undertaken extensive specific research into the genetic possibilities of color variation in the ferret.

It will be through the growth in popularity of pet ferrets that more color variation will be seen. Color mutations will tend to reflect the overall increase in the ferret population. The more of any species that are bred, the greater the chances of mutations occurring—though this does not mean we will ever see as many variations as in other species, such as rabbits. This is because it is still a matter of chance whether a mutation happens, and equally so whether it is recognized as such, and developed. It is also unlikely that the numbers of ferrets kept will ever compare with those of pets such as rabbits, guinea pigs, and mice.

All ferrets are born white and their color changes as they grow up.

THE NATURAL FERRET COLOR PATTERN

The ferret is a somewhat lighter color than the wild polecat. The underfur is beige. The longer guard hairs are almost white at their roots, steadily changing from cream, through yellow, to browns of varying degrees of darkness.

Some may even approach the almost iridescent blue-black of the wild polecat. The underbelly color is always lighter than that of the flanks and back.

The mask is very variable in its pattern, even within the same individual, depending on the time of the year (ferrets sport distinct summer and winter coats). The tips of the ears are cream or white, the extent of the tipping varying from one ferret to the other. In the summer coat the eyes are encircled by dark colored fur. There is a band of white or light colored fur above the eyes, and this becomes more extensive during the winter period. The muzzle is white or light in color, and there is usually a band of lighter colored hair on the sides of the base of the neck. The extent of the white muzzle is again extremely variable in ferrets.

The legs and tail are dark in color. The body may display varying amounts of lighter colored hairs. Overall, the color pattern is of an agouti type, the individual hairs being variably banded with color. The summer coat is both shorter and darker than that of the winter. The change from one to the other will commence during the spring and the autumn.

Such a change may take place quite rapidly, or over a longer period, so some ferrets may pass through a stage when they look rather ragged, with large handfuls of fur being shed. Those ferrets which most closely approach the wild polecat in color pattern are variously called either poleys or polecat-ferrets, not indicating a hybrid between the two. They are better called sables.

Between the dark and almost polecat color pattern, and that of the albino, there is an unlimited range of types. They are not, however, distinct varieties, because their genetic base is not as yet understood, other than in one or two obvious forms to be discussed. One ferret may display a dark mask, whereas another may have a totally white or cream face and upper neck. Another may be almost albino, but show some pigmentation on the legs and rump. The young ferret is of a darker color than the adult, the mature coat color being evident when the youngster is about three months of age. At subsequent molts the color of a ferret can change such that your ferret is never quite the same shade and pattern that it was in previous years.

COLOR VARIETIES

There are five basic color variations presently seen in ferrets. and they are as follows:

1. Sable. This has already been described and can be regarded as being of the wild or natural type.

2. Siamese. In this pattern the body color is rather lighter than in the sable. The mask, legs, and tail are similar in color to the sable.

3. White Feet or Mitted. In this variety, which is also called silver mitts, the feet are white, the extent of the white being very variable. There is usually some white in the form of a bib, and there may

Ferrets with differing masks. These came from the same litter.

be some white streaks on the head, body, and in the tail. The tip of the latter may also be white.

4. Silver. The silver is created by a reduction of color in certain of the guard hairs. Brown pigment is prevented from forming, thus giving the overall color a lighter hue and, in good examples, almost a silver appearance.

5. Albino. This is a pure white ferret with pink eyes. The albino lacks the capacity to form color pigment, the red of the eyes being the hemoglobin of the blood, not a color pigment. In some examples there may be a tinge of yellow seen in the fur.

In various areas you may hear of other varieties, such as white faced, sandies, broken coats, and similar terms which are used to describe certain individuals. It is likely that these are really only permutations, or extreme expressions, of the existing mutations, rather than being true breeding varieties. However, some of these variants can range from dark eyed whites to almost black ferrets, and these would strongly suggest that there are indeed a number of other mutations in the ferret just waiting to be systematically identified by geneticists. Once this happens, the potential scope for color development in the ferret will be considerable.

UNDERSTANDING BASIC GENETICS

At this time the vast majority of pet ferret breeders do not conduct planned breeding programs. It is more a case of their pairing whatever ferrets they happen to own, and hoping this will result in litters of fit and attractive looking pets. In the future there will be more breeders who will utilize genetic knowledge in order to develop colors and progressively superior stock. As this happens, so the ferret hobby will become more organized, and no doubt official standards of ferret excellence will be drawn up so that the ferrets can be exhibited just as happens in dogs, cats, rabbits and other pets.

APPLICATION OF GENETIC KNOWLEDGE

Genes are the units of hereditary—they determine all features of your ferrets from their color to their size, from their ability to resist disease, to their intelligence. Clearly, if you can manipulate these genes, you can improve your stock by bringing together those genes that are desirable, while removing those that are not. However, such manipulation is not easy in most instances due to the number and complexity of the way genes work. Further, while the genes themselves are the units of inheritance, there are many factors that also influence what a ferret will look like.

Genes give your ferret a very definite potential, but just how much of this is achieved will directly reflect environmental conditions. These include the way it is fed, its accommodations (cleanliness and scope to exercise), the stress level it lives under, and even the temperature. The temperature will influence color in particular. Additionally, the application of genetics has little value unless careful stock selection is practiced.

By combining all of these aspects, together with the keeping of detailed records, you increase your chances of success. What a genetic knowledge can do specifically is to act as a guide to what is and is not a prudent course of action. Further, by understanding basic genetic theory you are able to make a number of predictions about the outcome of giving matings, without having to actually conduct them. This can save a great deal of time—thus cost.

The limited state of genetic information with regards to the ferret is such that what follows is only a simple guide to how genes work. Certain of that discussed is factual with regards to the ferret, other aspects are speculative. But the underlying theory is the main thing to understand. This will allow you to try and interpret actual breeding results. In so doing you may be able to provide information that will ultimately enable geneticists to comment on the status of certain genes, those of color in particular.

MUTATIONS

Genes act in a very predictable manner, which is why offspring resemble their parents, at least in broad terms if not in detail. Two ferrets will produce other ferrets because the genes passed from each parent to their offspring are for ferret. However, when a gene suddenly changes in the way it expresses itself, it is said to have mutated. Such mutations thereafter also become very predictable in the way they express themselves. It is not fully understood what causes a gene to mutate, but the larger the population of a given species, the more likely it is that mutations will occur. When they do, they are either appealing, so are retained, or they are not, so are avoided. What one person considers appealing may not be so for another. This is why there are always some grotesque mutations retained in some pet species.

Popular examples of mutations in pets are longhair in a shorthaired species, such as dogs and cats, crests seen on

Because ferrets today are not scientifically bred following strict Mendelian genetics, they produce differing offspring. This lovely animal with a yellow face and neck, never became a *best seller*.

Produced without gene tracking, these three ferrets came from the same parents and all three have different masks.

certain birds, such as canaries and zebra finches, and all of the many color mutations seen in pets, those in the budgerigar probably being the most striking. It is convenient to use color as a working model of inheritance, because it is simple to explain. Single gene pairs often determine color, whereas for features such as size, or traits like aggression, the situation is much more complex.

HOW INHERITANCE WORKS

Each species has thousands of genes which collectively determine that it looks as it does. These genes are located in a linear manner on structures called chromosomes, which are found in all body cells. The chromosomes are always in similar pairs, except in the sex cells where one is shorter than the other. This pair determine aspects of sexuality. When reproductive cells are formed all of the paired chromosomes divide such that the sperms and the ova only contain one of the original paired chromosomes. At fertilization these single chromosomes are brought together, thus restoring the original paired situation.

The offspring thus inherits all of the genes that are on each chromosome, one of which came from the mother and the other from the father. A baby ferret therefore attains exactly half of its features from one parent and half from the other—never more from one than the other. If all of these genes are for the same expression the ferret looks just like both of its parents, given minor variations which is always seen in a species.

If, however, some of the genes received from one parent are of a mutated sort, this may change the appearance of the offspring. I say it may, because it may not, for reasons which will shortly be discussed, and which are the basis of genetics.

GENE LOCI

Before looking at genes in action it is useful for you to understand another aspect about genes. Taking color as an example (but the comments apply to all other features), there are many genes that control the color and pattern of this in your ferret. Each of these genes controls certain aspects of the color and its placement on the ferret. For example, one determines the amount of black in the hair, another the amount of yellow, another the density of the color, and yet another whether any color can in fact be formed at all. Yet further genes may simply vary the placement of the color, or may dilute it generally.

It works rather like a very complex control panel in which that seen is determined by which combinations of buttons are pressed. If all of the buttons are for normality, meaning the natural or wild state colors of the polecat, then it doesn't matter which combination you press the result will still be a 'normal' colored ferret. If some of the genes are mutated, then if those buttons are pressed the final color appearance may be changed.

THE ALBINO FERRET

What has just been discussed can be illustrated by considering the way an albino is created. The albino carries exactly the same number of color genes as a full colored ferret, with one major difference. In this instance none of the color pigments (brown-black and yellow-red) are able to form. The albino mutant genes suppress pigment formation, so the ferret is pure white. In the albino, both of the genes at what is termed the full color locus are for total suppression of color. However, if only one of the genes was for albino, and the other was for normal color, the ferret would be full col-

Albino ferrets are usually devoid of all black pigmentation.

ored—but would still be carrying the albino gene, which could thus be passed on to its offspring. If this offspring happened to mate with a ferret of similar genetic constitution, there would be a possibility of the two albino genes uniting in their offspring, when another albino would be the result.

GENETIC TERMINOLOGY

We can now introduce some genetic terminology into the discussion. You will need to learn this in order to develop your understanding of the subject. Two very fundamental terms are those of dominant and recessive. Genes can basically be divided between those which are dominant and those which are recessive in their action. What this means is that a dominant gene can express itself visually when present in only single form. A recessive gene must be present in double dose before it can be seen. What you can see in your ferret is called its phenotype, whilst the way such appearance is created is known as the genotype. A dominant gene is indicated in

Ferrets love to play and friendliness may very well be an inherited characteristic which can be genetically controlled.

genetic formulae by using a capital letter to represent the gene. A recessive gene is indicated by using a lower-case letter. Do remember that at each color locus there are two, and only two, genes present. One is on each of the paired chromosomes, and these were inherited one from each parent. Each locus at which a mutational form is known to exist can be given a letter to identify it, and this letter is usually taken from the mutant form.

In the case of the albino the letter would be a, denoting that it is a recessive gene. The locus is thus the albino locus. The full colored ferret would be identified with the letter A. However, as the alternative gene at this locus is for full color development, this locus is also often referred to as the full color locus, and is denoted with a capital C. In this case the albino would be identified as c. The use of the same letter for both genes at a given locus is so you do not forget that one is the alternative form to the other.

Using this information it can be seen that at the full color locus there are three possibilities:

CC CC CC

The first ferret has inherited two dominant full color genes (one from each parent), which is why its genotype is CC. The second ferret, with a genotype of Cc looks just the same as the first, that is, full colored, but it inherited an albino gene form one of its parents. It doesn't matter from which because the gene for albinism is not influenced by which sex carries it. The third ferret, with a genotype of

An albino strain in which only the black pigmentation is missing.

cc is an albino. To be such it had to inherit a gene for this color from each of its parents. Being in a double dose the gene c is able to function in suppressing the formation of color pigments, which it is not able to do when present in only a single form.

Such a gene is said to be epistatic in its action, meaning it is able to mask the presence of all other genes present in the animal that are responsible for color and pattern. We can now calculate what will happen when full colored ferrets are mated, one of which carries the albino gene. CC x Cc = CC Cc CC Cc

All of the offspring will be full colored, but half of them will carry the albino gene. These albino ferrets are called full color split for albino. This is written down as full color/ albino, that behind the line not being visual. There is no visual difference between any of these ferrets, so the only way to find out which were the purebred (for their color) and the non-pure, would be by a series of test matings. A pure ferret in terms of its color is said to be homozygous for this, one which is split is said to be heterozygous. The albino is thus a homozygous ferret, because the only color it can pass to its offspring is albino.

If ferrets with the genotype of Cc were paired the results would be thus: Cc x Cc = CC Cc cC cc

75% of the offspring would be full colored 25% of the offspring would be homozygous albino 25% of the offspring would be homozygous full color 50% of the offspring would be heterozygous full color.

In calculating expectations do remember that you determine what colors might be produced, not which will turn up in reality. There may be only two babies, so you could not have each of the four possibles. The two offspring would be one of the types that are theoretically possible, and the chances of which these would be have been calculated (i.e., a one in four chance of an albino and so on).

The genes combine in a random nature during fertilization, so you must calculate all possible combinations. In this last example each parent could pass either a C or a c gene to its offspring. These could unite with either the C or the c of the other parent, thus the four possible combinations. From this example you can appreciate that if you did not want to produce albino ferrets it would be important to know that the initial stock you purchased was not carrying the albino gene.

The dark eyed white ferret is not an albino. In this instance it is created (probably) by a dominant gene that

suppresses color formation in all parts of the body other than in the eye. The gene need only be present in a single dose in order to show itself visually.

SIAMESE PATTERN

If the Siamese pattern in the ferret is inherited in the same manner as that in the cat, the rabbit, guinea pig and other animals (it is called Himalayan in non-feline species), it means it is a

The white-faced ferret variety.

recessive mutation found at the full color locus. This means that at this locus there are three possible expressions: full color, Siamese, and albino. A ferret can only carry, at most, any two of these. It can thus be full color, full color split for Siamese, full color split for albino, Siamese, or albino. Siamese is written in formula by having a superscript above the c thus ^{cs}. If a ferret displaying the Siamese pattern was mated to an albino the result would be Siamese kits split for albino. Although the Siamese mutation is recessive it will act as a

dominant to the albino in this instance because both mutations are at the same locus.

CINNAMON (BROWN)

Should a light brown, or cinnamon, mutation appear in the ferret, which is very likely, if it does not exist already, the probability is that it will be created by a recessive mutation that reduces black pigment, or dark brown, to light brown. The eye color may become a dark ruby red, rather than black. Such a color will serve to illustrate another genetic point. This is in respect of what happens when two pairs of recessive genes, at different loci, are paired together. Let us pair a brown to an albino.

The brown ferret will have a genotype of CCbb. Its genes at the full color locus will allow full color expression. However, the genes at the black pigment locus have mutated such that the black is reduced to brown —so the full color expression is thus brown. The albino has the genotype of ccBB. The pigment at the black locus is not mutated, so it would normally allow for black (or very dark brown) pigment to be formed. However, the mutated genes at the full color locus prevent the expression of any color at all, so no black pigment is formed.

The brown ferret can pass to its offspring a gene for full color, and a gene for brown, thus the gametes are Cb. The albino can pass a gene for albino c, and a gene for black pigment B, thus its gametes are cB. The genotype of the offspring must therefore be CcBb, there being no other permutation possible. If you read this genotype to find out what the offspring will look like, the answer is that they will all be normal colored ferrets, but split for both brown and albino. The genes C and B are both dominant to the recessives c and b. Gene C calls for full color (whatever that is), while B is black, so the ferret displays both of these genes. It will pass on both the brown and albino mutant genes because both are located at differing loci.

Here we have an example of two different colored ferrets producing a third color variant. Once you understand how this comes about it can be very useful, as you will no doubt appreciate.

FUTURE COLORS

What colors might we look forward to seeing in the coming years? Based on those in other animals quite a few if the ferret continues to gain in popularity. An all black is an obvious possibility, as is a blue. A platinum could well be developed, as could a palomino. Each of these, together with gunmetal, sapphire, and other shades are will established in the mink. The piebald, or magpie, is a definite probability in terms of pattern, because these are merely variations on the spotted gene, which is already present in the ferret in the form of the white mitted (footed) variety. Creams are already present in a basic form, so it can be expected that these will become more refined. A red ferret is yet another possibility, while in terms of coat types I wonder what a rex coat would look like should it appear—as it has in many other small pets.

A satin coat is very likely, as is a longcoated mutation. These are not idle dreams, but very real possibilities that could turn up in your stock! As they appear, so they will add to the interest in this little mustelid.

RECORDS

It is essential that any serious breeder, indeed, even a casual breeder, should maintain accurate records of their breeding results. These should indicate the color of the parents, and the color of all the offspring. Any that are unusual should be brought to the attention of a geneticist in order that they can be studied and documented. The breeding records should also indicate how many offspring were born, how many died, at what age, and why (if this is known). The age of the parents should always be noted. The size and weight of the offspring can be monitored at differing ages, and in this way a complete history of the stock is built up.

This history will be crucial in planning future matings, and selecting that stock which is worthy of retention for breeding from. It will also pinpoint any ferrets that are producing less than desirable qualities, the latter including docility, a very desirable feature of a pet ferret.

STOCK SELECTION

Clearly, just how well a breeder does in any animal hobby will be determined not only by the general standards they maintain in terms of husbandry, but also in how good they are at making sound judgment in relation to stock retained for future

breeding. It is not as easy as you might think to select good breeding stock, because there are many ways to go about this.

You must first of all have a very clear mental picture of what you want in your stock in relation to size, color, and all other features. You must also be able to recognize faults, such as an over snippy jaw, or a short, or overlong back. Is the head size of your stock too large, or does it appear so because the body is too small? There are many problems in making these decisions, and even more in correcting them.

You must evaluate stock against written records in which the various strengths and weaknesses are listed and graded in terms of their relative importance. It is then essential that you asses stock in a consistent manner—and evaluate it at differing ages, because ferrets can get better or worse as they grow up. The highest priority of all must always be in respect of good health. There is no future to breeding from a super colored individual if it also has a record of passing on some problem to its offspring.

There are many disappointments for the serious breeder, and many compromises will have to be made when making selections. If your judgment proves correct, you will have the satisfaction of developing a much sought after line of healthy and beautiful ferrets. Read as much as you can on the subject of genetics, and on breeding methods and stock evaluation systems. You will find these fascinating and richly rewarding in helping your breeding program.

This magnificent strain of ferret has white front paws, brown rear paws and a white bib.

Ferrets are very hardy little animals but, like any other pet, they can fall ill to a great many conditions and diseases if they are not looked after properly. Preventative medicine is much more cost efficient, as well as being less of a worry to you, than having to treat a problem. All diseases, and most major conditions, cannot be diagnosed nor treated by the hobbyist, they will need the services of your veterinarian. Minor problems may well be treated at home if they are identified promptly, and not allowed to become the source of secondary infection. Often these prove to be far more dangerous than the original minor problem.

In discussing health care there are three broad areas to consider. The first is how the pathogens (disease causing agents) arrive in the ferret's home, and increase in numbers. The second is how a problem is recognized and diagnosed. The third is what treatments can be effected.

ESTABLISHMENT OF PATHOGENS

Harmful bacteria, viruses and fungi are transported to your ferret and its living accommodations by air, via food, and by being physically carried—either by people, by other pets, on equipment, or by other ferrets added to a collection. By appreciating these facts, and the inevitability of pathogens always being present around your ferrets, you can then see how you can limit their numbers to the degree that they can never become a major health threat.

In order to develop its immune system, a ferret must be exposed to bacteria at low levels so its body cells can recognize the pathogen. Once it has attacked the ferret in small numbers it is killed by the ferret's defensive cells and 'cataloged' for future reference. Over any given time period a pathogen may be 'forgotten' by the immune system. This is why injections, and subsequent boosters, are introduced to the ferret's blood system via injections for the major ferret killer diseases.

If the pathogens are only present in small numbers the immune system is able to deal effectively with them—so you never even know that this constant battle is going on. However, if conditions favor a dramatic increase in the population of the pathogen, or if the ferret becomes weakened for one of many reasons, then the bacteria are able to attack the ferret's body cells in the sort of numbers that the immune system just cannot cope with. It breaks down, and a condition or disease is the result. It then becomes a case of trying to find a suitable anti-pathogen to normalize matters, and bring about a recovery.

The prime areas of pathogenic establishment are as follows:

1. Accommodation: The sleeping quarters are easily invaded by parasites, bacteria, and fungi. They are ideal locations because they are dark, usually contain many crevices, and are warm. They also provide a constant source of food in the form of bedding, scraps taken by the ferret, and the ferret itself. Be very thorough in routinely cleaning the nestboxes. If they are of wood, assemble them with screws so they can be taken apart each year for cleaning. Always have a number of spares that can be left unassembled in daylight for a few months. Bacteria generally do not like strong sunlight. Cardboard sleeping boxes should be replaced on a very regular basis.

Outdoor ferret sheds should be cleaned weekly with a suitable disinfectant. Playthings should also be cleaned each week. Cage wires are a very common means of bacteria gaining access to your ferrets. The pet may chew on the wires, or wipe its muzzle on these. Litter trays should be cleaned daily. Again, it is prudent to have two or more trays so that one is always in an unused state on a rotational basis. Any that become chipped and cracked are best discarded. The same comments apply to food and water containers, as well as such items as spoons and other servers.

Be wary of creating piles of vegetation in the vicinity of outdoor ferret accommodation. In the warmer months it will be a bacteria's paradise! Fungi will also develop on this. The spores of these plants are extremely difficult to eradicate once they become established in the quarters of your pets. Ringworm, a skin condition, is caused by fungus, not a worm.

2. Food. Be sure all food is fresh. Do not leave moist foods, such as meats, mashes, and milk, down for more than the time it takes for your pets to eat their meal in comfort. These are easily colonized by pathogens carried in the air, or placed

onto the food as flies alight onto it. Replace water on a daily basis.

3. On the Ferret. If you notice your ferret has a minor skin abrasion or cut, this should be cleansed immediately. If parasites, such as lice or fleas are seen, these should be eradicated using proprietary treatments. The bites of these pests are both areas for pathogenic colonization, as well as a means by which such agents gain direct injection into the blood of your pets—from the blood sucking lifestyle of the parasites. You must always treat the ferret's accommodations once parasites have been seen. Repeat treatments are needed to destroy hatchlings from the parasite's eggs: the latter are rarely destroyed by the treatment.

QUARANTINING STOCK

An obvious way pathogens can be introduced to your stock and its accommodation, is via any additional ferrets purchased. To reduce the likelihood of this happening it is wise to quarantine all newly acquired stock, regardless of how good you consider the source of these was. The period of quarantine should be 14-21 days, which should be sufficient for any incubating diseases to manifest themselves.

The isolation quarters should be as far away from the main stock as possible. While under quarantine you can monitor the behavior and feeding mannerisms of the new stock. This is very important because often the first signs of an impending illness will be behavioral changes, together with a disinterest in

food. Also, while in isolation, you may decide to routinely treat the new additions with an anti- parasite spray or powder, as well as to worm them using a suitable remedy from your vet. The single pet owner adding another ferret may not feel quarantining one extra ferret is justified. This may well be the case as pets in the home are at far less risk to diseases than are numbers of ferrets in a breeding stud. Even so, it might be worthwhile keeping the new addition away from the resident ferret for a week or so, just to be on the safe side.

If you have a ferret breeding stud, it is advisable to wear a nylon overall when dealing with your stock. This material is not an ideal place for parasites to dwell on, when compared to normal clothing. You are also advised to wear disposable surgical gloves when handling either ferrets that are not well, or recently born youngsters. Always wash your hands after moving from one ferret cage to another —all of these little precautions will reduce the risk of bacteria being transferred by you from one ferret to another.

DISEASE RECOGNITION AND DIAGNOSIS

Diseases in animals may follow one of two paths. They may run their course with the animal showing no, or few, clinical signs of ill health. The first inclination you are given of a problem is finding the ferret dead. In such instances you should at least try to gain something from such an occurrence. The body should be taken as quickly as possible to your vet in order that

a post-mortem can be carried out. This may not reveal the cause of death, but then again it may, and will be worthwhile in that it may enable you to take a remedial course that will safeguard the rest of your stock.

One of the problems with pathogens is that they rapidly leave a dead host, so unless tissues and organs have been damaged by them, it may be impossible to determine events, so the diagnosis becomes death from non-specific causes.

If the disease or condition displays physical signs these will usually be one or more of the following:

1. Liquid discharge from the eyes or nose. Cloudy eyes. 2. Diarrhea, which may or may not be bloodstreaked. 3. Vomiting 4. Emaciation 5. Convulsions 6. Excessive scratching 7. Loss of hair 8. Swellings, abrasions, lumps, or sores. 9. Lethargy and a general disinterest in food. 10. Excessive thirst 11. Unusual behavior.

Some of the signs, such as weeping eyes and a runny nose, may be nothing more sinister than a common cold or chill. Vomiting may be simply to rid the body of something recently eaten in a gluttonous manner. All ferrets scratch from time to time, so the term excessive is a relative statement. Your ferret may go off its food for a day, just as you have days when you do not feel your normal bouncy self. In very hot weather all ferrets will tend to appear listless if there is no cool spot for them to recline in.

However, in all of these instances the ferret should return to normal behavior relatively rapidly, and certainly in no longer a time span than 36 hours. If after this time the ferret's condition has not improved, indeed, looks to have become worse, a vet is definitely needed. Clinical signs to a whole range of diseases are very similar, thus making home diagnosis a very risky undertaking. Even the highly trained vet may find it difficult to pinpoint a condition without recourse to microscopy of fecal or blood samples.

The best thing you can do if you are concerned is to list all of the signs that are giving you course for worry, then make notes on the total conditions as they are at the time. These will include the food your ferret is being given, how long the ferret has been owned, and whether any others of your stock are showing similar signs of illness. Examine the area around the accommodation, if it is outdoors, to see if there are any dead animals about—such as mice, rats or birds, and which may be the source of the problem. It is a case of doing as much detective work as you can so that questions asked by the vet can be answered, having already been asked by yourself.

TREATMENTS

The treatments available today for ferrets are comparable to those used in cats and dogs. Indeed, as the ferret suffers from conditions found in these two pets many of the treatments are identical, differing in dosage rather than type. The first thing that you should do if you suspect one of your ferrets is ill is to isolate it. Invariably heat

treatment will work wonders for minor conditions, such as chills. An infrared lamp suspended above one end of the cage will allow the patient to move away from the heat source if this becomes uncomfortable.

Heat lamps should be of the dull emitter type so that the ferret is not stressed by bright light. One advantage of isolating the ill patient is that it is removed from the general hustle and bustle of activity if it lives with a number of other ferrets. However, the isolation can also upset some ferrets if they have developed especially strong bonds with another ferret. This so, retaining the friend in the area of the patient may help to lessen any stress caused by the separation—pending the advise of your vet.

If a ferret is displaying diarrhea it is advisable to reduce the amount of meat given, or even give none for 24 hours, and not to supply milk at all. The condition should clear up within 48 hours, but if not you are probably dealing with something more than a simple digestive upset. Likewise, heat treatment will normally clear up a minor chill within 36 hours. If it persists then veterinary counsel is needed. Once the ferret has been isolated you can then contact the vet who may wish to see the pet. If heat treatment has been commenced it is important to ensure that the ferret is kept nice and warm in a box en route to the surgery.

Minor cuts and abrasions may ensue from hobs biting the neck of a jill during mating, or they may result from ferret squabbles, or cuts

caused by exposed weldwire edges. In all cases the wound should be cleansed with very mild saline solution, then covered with an antiseptic liquid, ointment or powder. We have found the liquid types very satisfactory. Bites from insects should be treated likewise—but keep your eyes on these in case they turn into an abscess, which will need veterinary attention. If there is a minor blood flow this can usually be stemmed by using a styptic pencil, or other coagulant.

During very hot weather ferrets may suffer badly from heatstroke. They will appear quite distressed, stretching themselves out on the floor and panting. As with a cat or dog suffering likewise, the immediate thing to do is to bring down the ferret's body temperature. You can soak a towel in cold water and wrap this around the ferret, replacing it periodically. Move the ferret to a cool spot, and try to give it some cold water. In an emergency hold the ferret and place it into a bath of cold water—but not its head of course! The head can be sponged carefully with water. Call the vet for further advice.

Should a ferret be frightened, bitten by a dog, or otherwise placed into a state of shock, it will collapse on the floor, its body temperature will fall, and its eyes will indicate its loss of consciousness. Move it very carefully to a quiet and darkened room. Place a blanket over it—but do not provide any other form of heat as this might prove counter productive. Talk soothingly to it, which may reassure it. Have someone call the vet promptly. Normally,

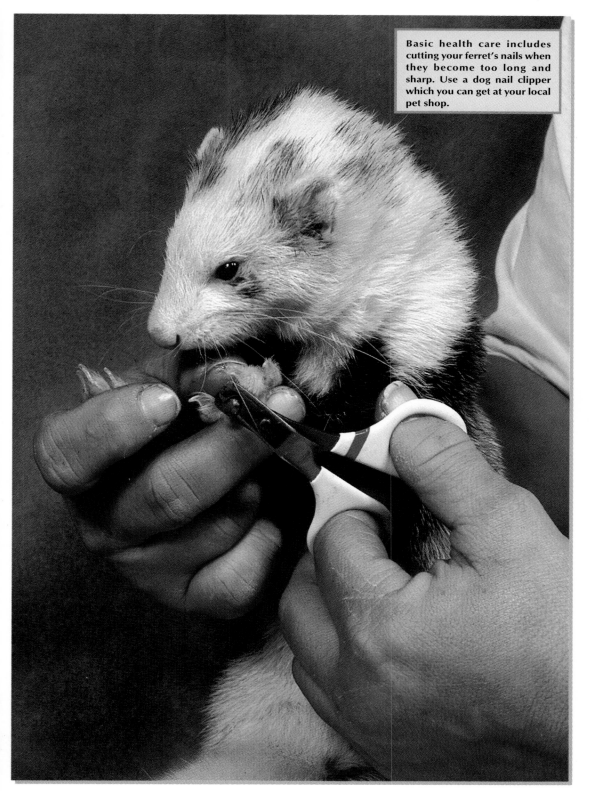

Basic health care includes cutting your ferret's nails when they become too long and sharp. Use a dog nail clipper which you can get at your local pet shop.

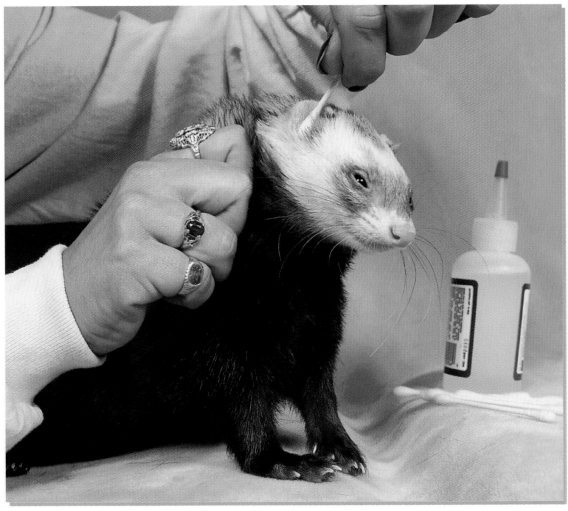

Cleaning your ferret's ears is part of the normal grooming process. Look for parasites while cleaning the outer ear.

after a while, the ferret will slowly recover its composure. Be aware that sometimes a state of shock may not occur for some minutes after the ferret has been frightened, so if you know that has happened, place it in a room as stated, just to be on the safe side.

The major diseases of ferrets, especially canine distemper, can be protected against by immunization, which can be done as soon as the ferret has been weaned. Up until then, it is afforded passive immunity by antibodies in the colostrum milk of its mother, assuming this has been taken within 24 hours of its birth. You should ensure your ferret is given full protection against the major diseases. Further, as discussed in previous chapters, pet ferrets should receive veterinary surgery in order to either safeguard them from risk of infections (spaying in the jill), or to make them more suit-

able as pets (vasectomy or castration in the hob).

If the advice given in this chapter is followed, and assuming the ferret is living under clean conditions, it should live a healthy and happy life. It will no doubt suffer some minor problems as it matures, but if these are acted upon promptly they will not develop into more serious complaints.

Most illness can be avoided by sound husbandry, or rapidly cleared up by prompt action, should they occur.